Uninstall Procrastination

How to Beat Chronic Procrastination and Get Things Done

Rob Regal

Table of Contents

Chapter 15: Tracking And Reviewing Your Progress

Conclusion

Introduction

Welcome to *Uninstall Procrastination,* the practical guidebook for you, the person who has installed the software of dread. That's right, *dread.* You know what I'm talking about. It's that feeling you get when you look up at the clock and realize you only have 15 minutes to get to work, yet you live 20 minutes away, or that panic that sets in when you look at the calendar and realize a big deadline is days away and you have done nothing to meet it. That churning feeling rises in your stomach as you know that the likelihood of you fulfilling your promises or desires is small at this point, even though it didn't seem like that big of a deal until right at that moment. Sure, you had hours, days, weeks, or even months to prepare and get it done on time, but you procrastinated because it seemed like other things were more fun or more important than that. Until now, when you realize how important it truly is, there is no way you will finish on time. *Dread.* Procrastination-induced, stomach-churning, embarrassment-creating, full-frontal *dread.*

It doesn't have to be like that. You know that, too, yet you cannot get yourself off the track you are on, so day in and day out, you succumb to the dread. Maybe it looks like a lost cause like you will never be able to get anything done because this is "just the way you are." You know that's a load of you-know-what, and I do, too. That's why it's time for you to stop making excuses, stop succumbing to procrastination, and start doing something about it.

Despite many believing that procrastination is a character flaw and there is nothing you can do about it, the truth is that procrastination is a learned habit. You did not sit in class, discovering how to make yourself sick to your stomach and embarrassed in front of the most influential people of your life by wasting your time playing video games or scrolling social media rather than working on essential priorities. You did, however, discover that doing those things seems way more fun than what needs to be done, and now you keep doing it. Mostly, you have installed a bugged software into your brain that is pretending to offer you one thing when, in reality, it is creating what you are trying to escape from. Now, you have to uninstall it to get to work, get things done, and live a life you are genuinely proud of. And still, play video games and scroll social media, because free time is essential, too.

You can uninstall procrastination by first understanding what procrastination is, why you do it, and how it affects your life. Being realistic about the severe consequences you face because of procrastination, ranging from damaging your reputation to keeping yourself trapped in a lifestyle with no growth, allows you to see how much your procrastination costs you. This way, you can decide once and for all if it is worth the price.

I'll tell you right now it isn't.

My name is Rob Regal, and I'm a health coach who has helped countless people overcome procrastination to get in the gym and meet their wellness goals. While my focus is specifically on helping people get into the gym and take care of their physical health, my strategies for overcoming procrastination has helped my clients in many other areas of their lives, too. Once you learn how to apply these practical strategies to one area of your life, you can do it repeatedly for every area of your life. Before you know it, you are no longer trying to avoid the work because you realize the value you gain from putting effort in is way more than the amount you gain from procrastinating. My clients have improved their physical wellness and advanced in numerous other areas of their lives, ranging from their careers to their family lives and even within their favorite hobbies and personal goals, all because of these skills.

Learning how to overcome procrastination is not about giving up on enjoying your life. You are not asking yourself to stop having fun, lose the thrill that comes from gratification, or create a rock-solid work ethic that keeps your nose to the grindstone 24/7. When you learn to overcome procrastination, what you *are* doing is learning how to delay gratification to get way more of it. The thrill you experience from achieving these big things in your life, whether it be handing reports in on time or finally launching that business or getting that six-pack you have always dreamed of, is 100x better than the thrill you get from popping a couple of zombies on video games or double-tapping a favorite celebrities latest post on Instagram. You just have to learn how to teach your brain to see the value in delayed gratification so you can easily stay on track with it for the long haul.

It isn't easy at first, I'll give you that. Every week I have clients calling me letting me know they want to quit working on their physical wellness for many different reasons. While I always respect someone's right to choose, before they finalize any decisions, I always ask, "Is this because you truly do not fit within the program, or is this because you are not feeling fired up by the results you have created so far?" More often than not, it is because they do not see instant results, and they begin to feel disappointed by that. They crave the instant gratification that we have come to accept as the norm in our modern world. I always remind them that they will *never* see those results if they don't keep trying, and more often than not, after a good talk about how to overcome those feelings, my clients re-commit to the program and see excellent results shortly after. Every single time, they tell me how grateful they are that I helped them overcome a limiting belief and breakthrough procrastination so they could create the results they had been looking for when they hired me.

I'm not saying that once you finish reading my book, you will have a six-pack, a new business, or anything else that you have been hoping for in your life. That's not the way this works. Just because you have taken those early steps does not mean the rest will be handed to you on a silver platter. What I am saying, though, is that if you read this entire book, start to finish, and apply the lessons I teach you, you will be taking practical and useful steps toward overcoming procrastination. Through that, you will have everything you need to get that six-pack, start the business, or accomplish your biggest dreams in life.

The thing is, you can't wait any longer. If you put this off or set this book down because you'd rather twiddle your thumbs or live vicariously through people on social media who are out there accomplishing incredible things, you will continue idling in life. You need to start minimizing your time invested in distractions and begin giving your all to your dreams, to reach them and live a life you love living, and you need to start *NOW*.

Are you ready? Let's go.

Part 1: Recognize The Virus

Chapter 1: What is Procrastination?

If something is not within your realm of awareness, there is nothing you can do about it. Think about it, if you were walking down the street and your friend was walking on the opposite side of the road, but did not see each other, would you know to wave hello? No, because you did not see each other. This is not an act of rudeness or an intentional snuff as you ignore your friend. This is a genuine experience driven by a lack of awareness. You were not aware that your friend was there. Therefore, you did not wave. Had you been informed, you likely would have waved or even gone over and said hello.

We cannot take action when we do not know that there is something to take action on. Likewise, if you know there is something to take action on, but you do not clearly understand what it is, you do not know what type of action to take because you are unaware of the solution to your problem. The fact that you are still procrastinating to this day is not a sign that you are incapable of change, but rather than you are unaware of how to change *your* reasons behind procrastinating. To diagnose your unique formula of procrastination, you need to understand what procrastination is and how it affects you on a practical level.

Procrastination – The Behavior

Behaviors associated with procrastination are primarily associated with evasiveness or avoidance. When you procrastinate, you are delaying taking action because, in your eyes, you don't want to or you don't need to take action right now. Rather than taking action, you start engaging in distractions and doing things that seem more important to you at the moment, even if, in the bigger picture, they hold zero importance whatsoever.

To yourself, procrastination is a readily justifiable behavior. It is usually justified by saying, "I have plenty of time" or "This is more important right now, that can wait." You might even explain purposefully missing deadlines or being late with things because of the consequences that seem more reasonable than the consequences of not engaging in your present distraction. At that moment, these all seem perfectly reasonable, and you believe that you will be fine dealing with the effects of whatever choices you have made, even though if you were to pause and reflect, you would quickly realize that they were poor choices.

Once you begin to reach the point where the consequences are about to be faced, your behavior likely starts to change. Suddenly, rather than being relaxed and passive about the entire thing, you begin to become stressed and anxious. The reality that you have chosen these consequences, either purposefully or as a by-product of recent behaviors, starts to set in, and you begin to realize precisely what that means for you. Your heart races, your palms get sweaty, and your mind begins to fly through all of the things you need to get done to achieve something meaningful toward your goal. The pressure becomes so heavy that it seems impossible to act. Now, you justify cutting corners, reducing your standards, and rushing as a way to try to avoid having to take such extensive consequences for the decisions you have made.

As soon as the actual consequences strike, you switch from stress and anxiety to embarrassment and shame. Now, you have to face your results, and you realize just how serious they are. They may not seem incredibly serious overall, but as they compound over time, they begin to feel worse. You have to face your loved ones complaining that you are late again, your boss writing you up for your final warning, or your friends giving up on inviting you because they are sick of you never following through. Or, worse, the deadline of a precious goal passes on the calendar, and you realize you have accomplished absolutely nothing, and there seems to be zero hope of you ever-changing your actions so you can do something you are proud of for once.

Over time, this cycle repeats so often that you almost become numb to the stress, anxiety, embarrassment, and shame. Only, it's not a real numbness, it's more of a tolerance that drives you to experience low self-esteem and low self-confidence, and that leaves you settling for less than what you truly deserve in life. You might stop making goals, arranging to do things, or agreeing to help others out even though you want to because you do not trust yourself to follow through. That lack of trust in yourself can have serious consequences, both in the relationship you share with yourself and the actions you take in life. The long term consequences of your procrastination are a life unchanged, unfulfilled, and unloved by the one who should have the most energy to pour into it and turn it into something magnificent. Rather than fulfilling your wildest dreams, you waste more time on distractions to avoid facing the constant disappointment that you, and everyone in your life, have toward yourself.

Procrastination – Your Brain

It is easy to observe the behavioral patterns of procrastination, which is why many falsely believe that if they were to improve those behavioral patterns, they would overcome procrastination. While behavioral changes are essential, they must accompany an understanding of and change the way your brain works if you will see any significant changes in your procrastination habits in the long run. Otherwise, you will always come back to procrastinating and find yourself feeling even greater levels of disappointment and shame around your actions.

When you procrastinate, three specific parts of your brain are responsible for encouraging you to engage in this behavior. The amygdala or the limbic system, the emotional brain, and the prefrontal cortex all work together to create this habit. They are responsible for the pattern taking root and becoming a problem in the first place. Procrastination occurs when you find something unappealing, either because it is frustrating, tedious, causes you anxiety, or perhaps because you routinely get poor results when you try.

When this occurs, you develop an emotional response in your limbic system, which tells your brain that the task is unpleasant and should be avoided. It creates a level of motivation and momentum against the job and toward avoiding it. This is an evolutionary response that is designed to prevent you from doing things that are not generally good for you, such as sabotaging all your friendships or eating something that seems to make you sick every time you eat it. By avoiding it, you feel better, or at least you avoid feeling bad.

As the amygdala promotes avoidance to cause you to stay away from things that may threaten your existence, your prefrontal cortex attempts to force you to ignore the negative feelings and move forward anyway. It argues that even though you are unhappy with the experience, from a logical perspective, it will have a high payoff, so you should just get to work and move on with it already. This creates a sort of argument within yourself where one aspect of yourself is resisting a task, while the other is arguing that it makes perfect sense to get it over with so you don't have to do it anymore.

If your amygdala is enlarged and is generally in control, you will often succumb to impulse rather than logic. This means you will routinely procrastinate because this is what your brain is essentially telling you to do. As you engage in procrastinating behaviors, your mind will argue that the task itself is the big bad animal trying to attack you. Still, once you get closer to the deadline, your observation will shift, and you will believe that the deadline is the big bad animal. At first, the task was more stressful than anything else, but as you got closer to the deadline, the deadline became even more stressful than the job. Many people mistakenly believe that this means they work better under pressure when the fact is that they are merely misinterpreting signals being sent by their brains.

Research suggests that if you can remove control from the amygdala and give it to the prefrontal cortex, you will have an easier time relying on logical decision making than emotional decision making. Then, when you find yourself at a point where you need to make a decision, you will have an easier time taking the logical answer that gives you the best long term payoff, rather than the emotional response, with a more significant long term consequence. That is precisely what I am going to teach you to do in this very book, and through that, you will discover how to get your brain and your behaviors on board with the change. Thus, you will have a significant impact on your long term ability to change.

Procrastination – The Virus

Procrastination can spread like a virus, from one area of your life to another unnoticed. It can start with delaying low-impact tasks that you deem unpleasant, like cleaning your room, etc. Then, you start to put off more significant tasks as delaying becomes more and more acceptable behavior to you. Before you know it, the procrastination virus has taken over your life.

However, the opposite is also possible. The more disciplined and focused you become in one area of your life the more those behavior patterns can spill over into all areas of your life.

*

Procrastination is, in its essence, the habit of putting things off until you cannot put them off any longer. It is repeated behavior that becomes stronger the more you practice it, and it is one that can lead to you having incredibly negative consequences in your life as a result. The more you waste your time, the less time you have since time is finite.

Some people argue whether procrastination is a behavioral trait, a learned characteristic, or a psychological condition. The common consensus is that procrastination is a failure to self-regulate, which leads to people facing many consequences in their lives. Regardless of what it is, it is something that can have a severe impact on your life. Through it, you can face many unwanted consequences that can drain the joy out of your life and leave you feeling miserable, anxious, and disappointed in yourself and the life you have created. You need to get a handle on your procrastination as soon as possible if you want to stop dealing with these consequences and start enjoying a higher quality of life, with far more to be proud of.

Chapter 2: How Procrastination Destroys Your Life

Pause for a moment and reflect on all of the ways procrastination has affected your life. I'll bet that within a matter of one minute, you can summarize several different ways that you have been affected by procrastination in varying degrees. The more you procrastinate, the more these consequences compound, and the worse they start to feel because it seems like you cannot seem to break free from this behavior and accomplish anything significant. Before you know it, procrastination starts to destroy your life.

Procrastination does not destroy your life all at once. Like most addictions, in this case, an addiction to a dopamine hit, procrastination strikes slowly and comes in with a vengeance. At first, you are just looking for a pick-me-up, and you take it by way of distraction, which gives you a sense of instant gratification. What an incredible rush that is. Before you know it, you are continually choosing distractions over essential tasks because you love how it feels to give in to these distractions and feel the rush of instant gratification. Over time, you find yourself giving in to every single distraction and accomplishing nothing, to the point where words like "unreliable" and "inconsistent" become your labels, and people stop trusting you and believing in you. These types of experiences can significantly damage your sense of self-worth, among other things, by making it seem as though you are incapable of being relied on or achieving anything significant. When you start comparing yourself to your peers, who seem to have no trouble getting things done, it can begin to wear on you, making it even harder for you to break through these behaviors and grow as a person.

Your Work, Your Work Ethic, And Your Success

While work is not everything, as humans, we take great pride in the things we accomplish. Being able to point at something tangible and say, "I did that" feels incredible, and it is precisely why we often have such competitive spirits. Even generally, non-competitive people will appreciate the opportunity to take pride in something they have accomplished and will accept the ego boost that comes with it. That type of fulfillment generally feels good.

When you procrastinate, your work, work ethic, and success all go down the drain. You fail to advance through your career, you do not give the level of effort that you could provide, and you fail to accomplish anything significant. Promotions go to employees who are giving it their all. New opportunities open up for those who make it evident that they will value and invest in those opportunities. Even simple things like praise and recognition vanish or turn into complaints and disappointment as people realize that you will always sit back in your seat and give the minimal effort required to accomplish things. They stop relying on you, asking you to help, or appointing you to anything important because they know you are not going to invest the level of energy required to fulfill that task. They may even fire you because they realize you are a liability to the company. After all, you cost more than you give back.

Personal successes are things every one of us takes pride in. Naturally, you want to develop plenty of reasons for you to be proud of yourself!

It's time to stop talking about something you fulfilled many years ago and relentlessly talking about your dreams and desires and focus on actually doing what you say you will do. Another significant side effect beyond a lack of raises, sucky work, and nothing to show for your efforts is that procrastination can have a severe impact on the way you value yourself.

In life, it is healthy to have pride in what you do. You were born to do something special, and you deserve to feel the satisfaction of actually fulfilling that something special. Humans love to figure things out, create things, and have tangible successes that we can point to and take responsibility for.

Working is not just about "doing it for the man" or "doing what you are supposed to," it is about doing something you take pride in and having something you can share with the rest of the world. When you work, you are using your brain to solve problems, create solutions, and design something that is well-worth your efforts. The entire point is to give your mind something positive to focus on so you can pour all of your mental and physical energy into something that you can later be proud of. The result is that you are more mentally, emotionally, and physically fulfilled.

Your Love Life, Friendships, And Relationships

Relationships offer a wonderful sense of value to your life. Humans are a communal species, which means we require human contact to survive, and that contact has to be positive if we will thrive in our lives. Relationships increase your emotional well-being, provide a sense of stability, teach you how to improve your social skills, offer security during tough times, and fulfill our carnal need to be a part of a community.

When you procrastinate, your behavior can seriously take away from the quality of your relationships. People stop relying on you, trusting you, spending time with you, or wanting to have any relationship because they grow tired of the constant let downs. Even if it seems minor to you that you are always late, incapable of remembering to bring what you said you would, or are continually failing to fulfill promises, it does not seem minor to the other people in your life. To the other people in your life, this suggests you do not value them or that which is essential to them, and when you stop valuing people, they stop caring. People want to be in relationships where they feel valued and trust the other person to respect, care, and appreciate them to show them that they are valued.

The more you procrastinate, the fewer people will rely on you or spend time with you. You might even find that you start to lose relationships altogether and that people start to judge you for the choices you make and the actions you take. This judgment can turn into labels and ultimately destroy your reputation, and it all stems back to the decisions you are making and the actions you are taking. You can't even blame anyone else because you *are* taking the steps that are earning your reputation. And you know this, so you start feeling incapable of change and trapped in this low reputation without an exact way out. Again, your self-esteem, self-worth, and self-confidence falter as you begin to wonder if all you will ever be is someone who continually lets down everyone around them.

Your Sense Of Self-Worth, Self-Confidence, And Self-Esteem

Beyond your work and relationships, procrastination can deeply scar the relationship you share with and the beliefs you have about yourself. As you start to see your peers reaching their goals and sharing positive relationships while your procrastination has alienated you, your ideas grow worse. Soon, you go from believing you can change to thinking you can't. You might start to believe something is fundamentally wrong with you and that you cannot do anything to remove yourself from this uncomfortable position. Perhaps you may begin to think you are a lost cause, or there is absolutely no hope for you ever to experience anything positive in your life ever again.

As these mental spirals continue, your emotional well-being can be severely damaged. This is where you often find people feeling exceptionally down on themselves and achieving nothing except for a laundry list of expectations they'll never meet, all of which makes them feel even worse.

The final blow strikes when they become so convinced that they will never change that they stop trying. Even if they were offered an exact way out, they would not take it because they genuinely believe they are a lost cause, they will never be able to fix their behavior and recover from all of the damage their choices and actions have caused. Ultimately, they stay entrapped in this belief, and until they choose to change it, they will always engage in procrastination and other self-sabotaging behaviors.

Your Future Is The Price You Pay

The ultimate destruction that self-sabotage delivers is the high price that comes with procrastinating. That is the price of your future. When you engage in chronic procrastination, you decide that every dream you have ever set for yourself is meaningless and never fulfills those dreams. Rather than being a doer, you will always be someone who talks about what they wish to do and who achieves nothing. Never mind the embarrassment you feel when you let everyone know that you still have not managed to get ahead in life and remained trapped in the same cycle for years. What about the embarrassment you will feel within yourself?

How will you feel when the dates on the calendar pass, and you are still not any further ahead in life? Will you feel proud that you always have nothing to show for the days gone by, or will you wish you had started sooner? Will you convince yourself to start, or will you keep falling mercy to the cycle and lingering in the pit of shame year after year? How about when everyone surpasses you and achieves their dreams, and you are still only talking about yours? How have you already felt when all of these things happened to you? Probably not very good.

It's time for you to realize that the cost of procrastination is too high. You need to stop paying it and start investing your energy elsewhere to make your dreams come true. Like with getting out of financial debt, this will require you to realize that you are presently running in a deficit as far as your energy and credibility go. Once you start learning how to redesign your energy budget, you will find yourself efficiently investing in areas of your life that will get you ahead, and through that, you will experience greater joy. It is entirely possible and within your reach. All you have to do is start.

Chapter 3: The Real Reason You Keep Procrastinating

"You are under no obligation to be the same person you were 5 minutes ago." – Alan Watts. Have you ever wondered how you could recover your reputation and relationships after all of the mistakes you have made until now? Perhaps you and everyone around you believe you are lazy, and it is because of your unwillingness to change that you have completed all the mistakes you did. While you should take responsibility for these mistakes, it is essential to understand that your laziness is not the right place to blame. Procrastination is.

The real reason people procrastinate is far more complicated than laziness. The reason why people *keep* procrastinating is even more challenging than that. Understanding these reasons will help you feed your prefrontal cortex with the logic it requires to justify, in a productive way, why you have engaged in this behavior for so long. Once you understand that there was a reasonable cause behind it, you can also begin to fix that root cause and build trust that these behaviors will never come back again. If they were to, you could witness them immediately and start taking practical steps to reverse the effect and go back to the point of being in control once again.

The Number One Leading Cause Of Procrastination

Many people believe the number one leading cause of procrastination is laziness. It's not. The number one leading cause of procrastination is fear. People who procrastinate are often experiencing massive levels of anxiety in many ways, and those fears make them feel averted to engaging in the job that is driving the fear. For some people, there are only a few tasks that drive those fears. For others, many or even every task may drive those fears.

Those fears usually represent themselves as a fear of not seeing a reward for their efforts, indecisiveness, overwhelm, anxiety, task aversion, perfectionism, a fear of negative feedback, or a fear of failure. You might feel worried that if you were to put energy into this task, it would turn up fruitless or would create some sort of negative impact on you, and so you avoid engaging in the job whatsoever. This way, rather than dealing with those adverse effects, you can just deal with the negative impact of staying in one place. Often, that negative impact that comes with staying in one spot feels less invasive because you are already familiar with it, so it feels comfortable. Even if you are not truly happy with where you are at, you know what the pain feels like, and you are aware of what to expect here, which makes it easier for you to embrace that particular spot. If you were to make any changes or make an effort toward anything you want to accomplish, your circumstances would change, and you may fear that you would not be ready to handle the changes that come with them. Perhaps they would hurt more, be less comfortable, or would be too much for you to feel. So, you refrain from taking action because you do not want to face these possibilities.

Self-Sabotage Is A Major Contributing Factor

Self-sabotage, or self-handicapping, is a behavior people often engage in when there is a strong negative emotion or a negative belief surrounding a task. These might be: fear of failure, perfectionism, feeling unworthy, or simply fear that they will not be able to deal with the consequences (fear of the unknown). This could be intentionally sabotaging their ability to create specific results, receive opportunities, or otherwise fulfill their goals and desires. The sabotage they engage in is generally so well-crafted that they can shift the blame to others. In many cases, people who engage in this behavior even believe it themselves. Self-sabotage can become such a deeply ingrained behavior that people are entirely unaware of what they are doing, and sometimes even unwilling to reflect and admit to what they have been doing. Despite having the facts staring them straight in the face, they may believe that they have not been doing this because they have done such a great job justifying it.

When someone engages in procrastination as a form of self-sabotage, it can almost be guaranteed that they are engaging in other types of self-sabotage too. Procrastination may be just one of the ways. Different ways commonly include assuming things will go wrong and then behaving in a way that essentially forces things to go wrong, creating self-fulfilling prophecies in the worst way possible. They may also intentionally start acting strange or different in specific circumstances, such as by being rude to new people when they are generally lovely, as a way to fulfill those self-fulfilling prophecies.

If you are procrastinating as a form of self-sabotage, you need to dig into why you are self-sabotaging while also digging into the roots of your procrastination. The cure to both behaviors lies somewhere in the reason as to why these things are happening, and you have to discover those reasons and fix them. Finding the roots of your self-sabotage is best achieved through reflection and tracking. Do this by taking a journal and writing out every time you recall procrastinating in the past, then ask yourself why you started procrastinating at that moment. Then, start tracking your active bouts of procrastination and honestly answer *why* you are procrastinating. You will begin to see patterns around your procrastination that allow you to understand where this behavior comes from, and then you can use that to help you correct it.

Usually, when people become aware of their self-sabotaging behavior, that in itself allows them to stop engaging in it, as they can catch themselves at that moment.

Actual Disorders May Have Something To Do With It

For some people, actual disorders can lead to procrastination. In this case, procrastination is more of a symptom of a larger problem. Some of these disorders may lead to self-sabotage in general, so if you experience an array of self-sabotaging behaviors and cannot seem to easily overcome them, it may be ideal to ask your doctor in case something else is going on.

Attention deficit disorder (ADD) and attention deficit hyperactivity disorder (ADHD) are two examples of conditions that can lead to people procrastinating. With these particular disorders, it can be incredibly challenging to focus on a single task for any period, particularly if that task gets boring. In this case, you might find yourself jumping from task to task, never completing anything, and procrastinating going back to the original job you abandoned previously.

In addition to ADD or ADHD, anxiety, depression, trauma-related disorders, and even physical disorders can also result in procrastination because they make completing tasks much more challenging. For mental-related issues, it may feel particularly challenging to cope with any of the symptoms you are having as you attempt to complete important tasks, so instead, you put those tasks off. With physical-related issues, you may not be able to complete all of the physical tasks primarily associated with something, or you may not be able to do as much as you would like at once, so it feels easier just not to do anything at all.

Fortunately, even if you are dealing with a disorder that leads to you procrastinating, there is still plenty that you can do to help you stop. The first step is to start communicating with your doctor, as they can help you address any challenges unique to your situation. After you have talked with your doctor, you can also work toward applying the very skills described in this book to your situation, too. It may take longer or look different from how you imagined it. Still, if you remain focused on creating a positive outcome, there is always the opportunity to find something that works for you, so you can stop procrastinating once and for all.

Your Perceived Benefits Keep You Addicted

Once you have begun procrastinating, regardless of what the reason is, you start to imagine that your benefits are worthy of remaining trapped in this particular cycle. Or, at the very least, you use them to justify why it is okay that you are entrapped during this cycle if you cannot seem to get yourself out of it. The perceived benefits of procrastination are addictive because they are instant. They provide you with a rush in your mind that is similar to what you get when you consume an addictive substance, like sugar or intoxicating substances.

 The rush you get in your mind is a rush of dopamine, and that dopamine floods your mind with a feel-good sensation. Essentially, your brain rewards you for engaging in the instant gratification route rather than the delayed gratification route. This rush tells your brain that you have done it the right way and that you should keep doing things this way to continue experiencing that rush. So, you do. Thus, you find yourself experiencing a real addiction to these forms of instant gratification, whether it be video gaming, scrolling your phone, playing a game on your device, or feeding curiosities by looking up random questions, or anything else. As long as it can serve as a distraction that makes you instantly feel satisfied, it is instant gratification, and it is serving your addiction.

The longer it takes for you to become aware that your brain has become addicted to the dopamine rush associated with instant gratification, the more challenging it will be for you to heal that addiction. You must face the reality that you are addicted to these distractions if you can practically eliminate them from your life and carry on more healthily. This is because, once you have admitted the reality, you become aware of how your brain is behaving, and you can understand why you feel the way you do anytime you are faced with a decision to procrastinate or get things done. This makes restoring power to your prefrontal cortex, rather than your amygdala, far more effective. Thus, you learn to stop procrastinating by taking back control.

A Lack Of Knowledge Around How To Change Keeps You Trapped

Knowledge is power. With procrastination, very few people know about what is going on within themselves, and what drives this behavior to continue. If you have been trapped in procrastination cycles for any period, you know that it is not an easy one to break. A lot of misinformation has flooded society regarding what procrastination is, why you do it, and why it is challenging for you to stop doing it. The reality is that few of these resources hold any merit. Most of them point the finger at you and encourage you to blame or shame yourself in a way that limits your ability to change or worsens the cycle itself, rather than offering the tools you need to change.

Once you start to understand the cycles associated with procrastination clearly, and precisely what is happening with each stage, as well as the antidote to these stages, it becomes easier for you to fix them. You begin to find practical cures for the urges, frustrations, and pressures you feel within yourself that motivate you to behave in a certain way. At first, it will continue to feel challenging to engage in these new behaviors and maintain them so that you can shift your experience of gratification and improve your circumstances.

You might find that the first one or two times you make the change, it is fine, but after three or more times, you begin to feel a deep desire to slip back into old patterns. This is because your brain is now fully over the novelty of the change and wants to go back to what is comfortable and what delivers the biggest rush of dopamine. Remember, it is craving instant gratification. When you change your behaviors seemingly overnight, it experiences a momentary fulfillment of instant gratification from the change itself. However, as soon as your brain realizes that change requires you to delay all other forms of gratification, it starts to reject the idea and pushes you to go back to the "old way." You *must* keep applying your new approaches until you move through this.

As you continue to apply these changes and work through this knowledge in practical application settings, you will find yourself gradually overcoming procrastination. It may seem slow at first, but the momentum will pick up, and you will find yourself moving forward with your changes, and before you know it, procrastination will be a thing of the past. Remember, even a 1% change every single day leads to a 365% change in a single year. Small changes may not look like much at first, but they add up rapidly if you remain committed and see them all the way through. They are also the most sustainable, so when you make your changes this way, you become less likely to revert to your old way of doing things because you changed in alignment with the natural flows of your body and brain. If you find yourself returning to old patterns, getting back on track with your new changes will get you where you need to go.

Chapter 4: Taming Your Inner Critic

Your inner critic plays a more significant role in your life than you may realize. Procrastinators tend to have extremely critical inner voices that will relentlessly remind them of the many mistakes they are making, and the price they are paying to make those mistakes. They often use instant gratification. The dopamine rush to experience an immediate sense of relief from the negative feelings associated with the inner critic, which allows them to feel better even if only for a short while. Unfortunately, this also leads to them engaging in behaviors that turn out negative results, which makes it feel as though that hostile inner critic is telling the truth about how bad they are in life. Learning how to break free from this cycle allows you to stop running from your inner critic and facing harsh consequences from the never-ending marathon to give yourself the freedom you need to change. Fortunately, breaking the cycle and improving your inner voice is easier than it sounds, and you are a lot more motivated to make this change than you may already realize. After all, who wants to live with a bully strapped to them 24/7? No one. It's time to permanently eliminate your bully using a more positive escape so you can set yourself up for success.

Why Is Your Inner Critic So Harsh?

Have you ever had or witnessed someone who experienced a coach who used critical language to motivate their students to succeed? Perhaps they were blunt, routinely pointed out people's flaws, and came across as harsh or even in a bullying tone when trying to get people to stop engaging in certain things to become more successful?

We believe that if we lay on the negative attention, people will be motivated to *stop* doing something because they will not want to receive negative attention. Over time, it becomes challenging not to become harshly critical of everything because you focus on everything you don't want. Plus, you are not focused on what you *do* want, which means even if you change your actions, you may still be doing the wrong thing. The result is almost always people who feel a lowered sense of self-esteem and who have low morale with the person talking to them this way.

The same thing can happen inside of yourself. Your inner critic does not want you to make mistakes, make the wrong choices, or do something that could hurt you in any way. This is not exclusive to physical pain, either, but also the emotional or mental pain of rejection, harsh judgments, or anything else that could come from within yourself or those around you. To protect you from doing it wrong, your inner critic applies negative attention to every mistake you make. The problem is, before you know it, it seems like everything is a mistake, and you have not given yourself any positive sense of direction for what to do instead. Thus, you just keep laying it on.

Switching up the type of guidance you are giving yourself so that you are applying positive attention to the things you do want, rather than negative attention to the things you don't wish to, is far more effective.

When you apply attention to the positive things, you motivate yourself to do more of those and to look for more positive things you can do to create the results you need or desire. You can also start to look for positive ways to switch the negative things you are doing, which means not only will you stop engaging in these unwanted behaviors, but you will also start engaging in things you would prefer to engage in instead. This way, you are not criticizing yourself for everything you do, including your attempted changes. Instead, you are celebrating yourself for everything you do and discovering more ways to make things to celebrate about.

Create Space For Positive Conversation

Creating space for lively discussion within yourself is not something many people consider doing. It may come naturally to pick up the phone and text or call a loved one or plan to visit and enjoy a positive discussion with the people you care about. With yourself, however, it may seem like a strange concept to intentionally schedule a time where you can sit and have conversations with yourself. These conversations provide you with the opportunity to share positive discussions with yourself while also creating positive dialogue around any critical conversation that comes up in the process.

To engage in this habit, start by scheduling time to sit down and think about whatever may be pressing on you lately. Allow yourself to begin in whatever way comes naturally for you, then work on guiding that inner conversation toward something positive and productive. For example, if you have been upset about the way you behaved in a specific circumstance lately, you may want to think about that so you can bring closure to it. At first, you might naturally be harsh toward yourself and want to bully yourself for that behavior. Still, as you guide it toward a more positive conversation, you may focus instead on understanding why it happened and how you could have handled yourself better. Creating this positive shift means you can address the issue you are facing within yourself in a way that allows you to decide on a solution so you can feel confident that you will not behave that way again. Or, if you catch yourself behaving that way, you can work toward implementing the positive change you had already decided upon during your conversations with yourself.

If you do not have any pressing issues during one of your scheduled conversations, consider spending that time saying nice things to yourself, instead. This pep talk could include celebrating the positive changes you have made, cheering yourself on for the growth you are embodying, and allowing yourself to feel proud of who you are becoming genuinely. These positive check-ins are a wonderful way to continue to build a definite bond with yourself so that when pressing issues do arise, you are more likely to speak kindly to yourself and be forgiving with yourself for any mistakes you may have made.

Listen To What Your Inner Voice Is Really Saying

When your inner voice is being particularly harsh, it can help to pause and try to understand what it is saying to you. Often, the inner voice can grow harsh because it is so afraid of you experiencing pain again that it tries to fight you about situations with perceived threats. The harshness then is a mask for the problem you are feeling, and a defensive mechanism that ultimately says, "I am scared."

If you pause anytime, your inner voice gets particularly critical and seeks to understand what it is trying to protect you from. You can develop greater awareness around yourself and why you behave the way you do. You can also start looking for solutions for how you can successfully navigate the problem your inner voice is having without causing more pain to yourself. For example, your inner critic might be blocking you from trying something new for fear of you being bullied for making a mistake, because, in the past, you were bullied for any errors you made when learning new skills. In this case, you are afraid of judgment and bullying. By acknowledging this, you can affirm that things are different now, or adjust your environment to eliminate bullies or those who are likely to harshly judge you for mistakes you make during the learning process. This way, you are protected from what your inner voice is trying to save you from, *and* you can continue working toward whatever is meaningful for you.

Visualize The Success You Desire And Affirm It

A great way to encourage lively conversations within yourself is to visualize the success you desire and affirm that success to yourself. Spend time invested in daydreaming about what it is you truly desire in life, and let yourself become fully immersed in these daydreams, while also affirming to yourself that you are worthy and capable of fulfilling these dreams.

This may seem like a frivolous way to spend your time, but it has tangible benefits. When you visualize your dreams coming true, your brain does not realize that you are merely visualizing and not experiencing this reality. While your prefrontal cortex can remain aware of this, the parts of your mind associated with feeling and memory are not. This means that you are essentially priming yourself for positive experiences by teaching your brain how to accept them as an everyday occurrence and showing yourself how you can positively enjoy them.

If you spend this time visualizing everyday experiences, going well, you teach your brain to accept this as being normal. Thus, when you find yourself in these everyday experiences, you are more likely to feel confident in them, you will be more productive in your actions, and you will be far more positive in the conversations you share with yourself during those moments. This will all work together to create positive inner dialogue as well as positive external changes, such as minimizing your tendency to procrastinate.

It is essential, however, to avoid indulging in daydreaming too much. For procrastinators, daydreams can become problematic because they can provide false sensations of accomplishment when, in reality, you have yet to do anything. The best way to avoid your daydreams becoming problematic is to set a specific timeframe around how long you will allow your visualization to last, and being strict about ending that visualization and moving into action at the end of that timeframe.

Write Down Your Negative Thoughts

Sometimes, your negative thoughts just won't leave you alone. Keeping them bottled up inside may make it even more challenging to remain positive because, on a deeper level, you find yourself thinking and possibly believing in these inner conversations. Having a book where you can write down your negative thoughts gives you a fantastic opportunity to get them out of your head, so it feels as though you have fully expressed them. This way, you can start to bring closure to these thoughts.

A great way to start bringing closure to the negative thoughts is to read them after you have written them down. Start by understanding why they exist, what they are saying, and how they affect you. Consider what it would be like if you said this to another person, and ask yourself if you would ever truly talk this way or believe these things about anyone else in your life, especially people you love and care about. Chances are, you will discover that these negative thoughts are trying to protect you, yet they are doing it in a way that would be considered inappropriate if they were being said to anyone other than yourself. This is a pretty good sign that they are unsuitable to be saying to yourself, also.

The more you can work through your thoughts, have compassion for why they exist, and call yourself out on ideas expressed inappropriately, the easier it will be to start creating boundaries with yourself. Stop allowing yourself to talk to yourself in this way, and start holding yourself to higher standards. Expect that you speak to yourself with kindness, respect, and a clear intention to have a positive and productive outcome, rather than one that merely increases the problems you are dealing with. This way, you can start asserting these boundaries and maintaining them with yourself, which will allow you to start speaking more kindly and gently toward yourself.

Keep Practicing Using Your Positive Inner Voice

Lastly, you have to keep practicing. A pro basketball player doesn't get to their league by giving up on practice and expecting to play like a pro on the court. A master chef does not refuse to spend any time learning to cook, then expect to know how to cook gourmet meals on the fly. People who grow their skills do not refuse to work on them and then expect those skills to be efficient enough to call on those skills. Likewise, you cannot expect your positive thinking to suddenly kick in when you need it to if you have never practiced positively talking to yourself.

It is essential to understand that your cheerful inner voice may, at times, need to become a *productive* inner voice. Sometimes, you may use positive self-talk to justify your procrastination, rather than motivate yourself into action. The minute you notice yourself exploiting your cheerful inner voice to justify inaction, you need to focus on having a constructive inner voice. Your productive inner voice should still be bright and kind. However, it should also be more direct and aggressive. You need to be willing to call yourself out and hold yourself accountable, even when it's challenging, as this will keep you in action.

Chapter 5: The Stress Factor

Stress can create a great deal of trouble in anyone's life. Even though stress in and of itself is not problematic, many people find themselves experiencing excessive, prolonged stress, which begins to create issues in their lives. This prolonged, problematic stress can encourage unhealthy behaviors that drive greater levels of stress, as well as many unfortunate physical, mental, and emotional side effects. In fact, stress has been reported as having played a vital role in developing chronic or fatal illnesses in a significant number of people over the last century.

When it is operating effectively, stress applies that added pressure you require so that you can summon the energy, courage, and strength to get through anything you are facing. For example, if you are walking down a busy road and a bike starts riding quickly right at you, you will begin to experience stress as your body summons the energy, courage, and strength to get out of the way of the biker. From an evolutionary perspective, appropriately experienced and expressed stress has a positive impact on your overall well-being. Inappropriate stress, however, can be entirely problematic.

For many people, inappropriate stress is responsible for their experience of procrastination, which in turn leads to even more inappropriate stress. This cycle can lead to you feeling trapped in your behaviors because it seems too stressful to stop engaging in them, yet it is stressful for you to keep engaging in them, too. The catch 22 here is that the more you engage in these problematic behaviors, the more stressed you become, and the less you can handle that stress over time. However, the energy it takes to *stop* engaging in these behaviors can exert stress on your mind, emotions, and even your body as well, which makes it feel like that is a challenging route to take, also. To break out of this cycle, you have to realize that your long term stress will be broken if you stop procrastinating and take on the short term stress that comes with breaking this habit. It may feel strange or foreign, or it may even seem like a greater amount of stress in the present moment, but in the long run, it will lead to massive relief from the stress you have been facing. Even so, there are still many steps you may have to take to minimize your stress and break free from this cycle once and for all.

Stress Will Always Hold You Back

First and foremost, you need to understand that any amount of lingering stress will hold you back from experiencing success. Regardless of whether you are trying to break free from procrastination, reach your desired fitness goal, excel in your career, or otherwise advance in one way or another if you are chronically stressed, you will be holding yourself back. Having a good stress management practice in place will ensure that you can minimize your stress and keep yourself on track with all of the positive changes and achievements you are working toward.

A significant step toward the success you can take right now is to commit to seeing stress for what it is from this day forward. Stress is not a small, normal, unavoidable part of everyday life. Despite the fact that chronic stress is one of the most common experiences of our modern world, it is not a natural state to be in, and it is certainly not something to take lightly. If you experience chronic stress or *any* stress, you need to take that stress seriously and make it your number one goal to eliminate that stress from your life. This way, you have the energy and courage you need to carry on, and the pressure does not linger in the background wreaking havoc on your life.

Physically Move Your Stress Out

A profound statement I heard at one time or another was that emotions are energy in action. Stress is an emotion, which means it is an energy in motion in your body. The trouble is when people become stressed out, and they tend to do the opposite of move. Instead, they sit around and let their minds race while their bodies remain still or succumb to fewer movements. When invited to do something like go out with friends, exercise, or otherwise get moving, a stressed-out individual will often say, "No, thank you, I'm too stressed." Or, they will make an excuse, but deep down, the real reason is they feel too stressed, and they believe they will not feel good if they attempt to do something physically.

Remove the idea from your mind that you need to be happy and in a beautiful mood to get moving or to spend time in motion. Just because you are stressed does not mean you need to reject your schedule, skip out on exercise classes, or reject invitations to move with your friends. Go for that walk, hit the gym as you planned, or commit to checking in for the class you signed up for weeks ago regardless of how you are feeling. Once you get there, physically moving your body will allow you to move that energy right out of your body, allowing your stress to make its way out. As far as procrastination goes, if you find yourself saying no to getting started with a particular activity, commit instead to standing up and exercising for five minutes on the spot. Jog, do jumping jacks, stretch, or even just go for a quick walk around the block. Then, see how motivated you feel to get started with the necessary task.

Maintain A Nourishing Diet

Stress does a number on your body, especially when you hold onto it. It takes a lot of energy out of your body just to experience the emotion and accompanying physical symptoms of stress. If you want to move stress out of your body, you need to be aware of stress and take extra care of your body during stressful periods to recover rapidly. Not taking adequate care of your body during stressful periods can lead to more stress, as your body does not have the necessary resources to recover from the taxing effects of stress. This means you need to consume proper nutrition, as well as stay well-hydrated.

In addition to being intentional about eating a healthy, well-rounded diet, ensure that you are not relying too heavily on sweets or other foods that are commonly consumed when people are stressed. These can add more stress to your body and make it even harder for you to recover, even if you are eating a healthy diet at the same time. While you can still have sweets, consume them intentionally and in moderation.

It can also help to consume foods that are excellent for managing and recovering from stress in particular. Healthy comfort foods like oatmeal, nuts for snacking on, chicken soup, complex carbs, and foods rich in vitamin C, and omega fatty acids are excellent during periods of high stress. You can also reach for teas made with herbs like chamomile, lavender, peppermint, lemon balm, or passionflower, all of which are excellent at helping ease your nerves and relax you during difficult times.

Spend Time Having Genuine Fun

The saying that claims "laughter is the best medicine" actually holds a high level of merit. Laughter helps minimize your stress in two ways, both of which can have an immediate and profound impact on your well-being. First, when you laugh, you are expending a great deal of energy, which means any pent up energy that has been accumulated through stress can be laughed right out of you. It is similar to exercising to eliminate the stress, except you are doing so through laughter. This is why many people report laughing when it is inappropriate to be laughing, such as at funerals, because their bodies are instinctively moving the energy out and away from their bodies.

Second, laughter supports you through a process known as biofeedback. Biofeedback means that your brain receives signals from the sensations within your body. This is constantly happening, whether you are aware of it or not, and you can intentionally hijack the system to send messages to your brain to let you know that you are okay. Laughter is an excellent way to do so. When you hold yourself in a relaxed posture, maintain a peaceful facial expression, breathe at a slow rhythmic pace, or allow yourself to lay down and relax, you are letting your body know that it is safe for you to calm down. When you laugh, you also tell your body that it is safe to calm down and feel in a favorable, feel-good position. This way, not only does your body stop stimulating the stress response, but it also starts stimulating the production of serotonin and other feel-good hormones within your body. The result is that you experience relief from your stress!

Give Yourself Time To Deeply Relax

If laughter is a form of biofeedback, you cannot get behind right now. Consider giving yourself time to relax deeply. Sit back on the couch, dab a few drops of lavender oil on the back of a rice cushion, and lay it over your eyes (with the essential oil on the side opposite your skin and eyes to avoid injury), and place your hands over your abdomen. Spend time breathing using the 4-7-8 breathing rhythm, allowing you to let your body know that it is safe, and it is time to wind down and relax. To breathe this way, simply inhale through your nose for a count of four, hold it for a count of seven, and exhale for eight. Do this five to ten times, then return to a natural breathing rhythm for about two minutes. Continue this cycle until your natural breathing rhythm is calm, and you are feeling more relaxed.

Scheduling consistent time for deep relaxation, or even meditation sessions, has been shown to have incredible results on your overall stress and anxiety levels. When you give yourself time to relax and release tension intentionally, you start eliminating the lingering reserves of pressure to not feel like you are holding on to so much. Over time, you have calmed yourself enough that you can feel at peace within yourself, and even new stressors do not feel as complex to navigate because you are not already carrying so much with you. Thus, you feel a great sense of ongoing relief from stress in your life.

Talk It Out With Someone Who Cares

Sometimes, straight old talking is the best way to get through a stressful time. Venting to someone who loves you and who will be nonjudgmental and compassionate toward you is an excellent way to get your stress out and find closure from all the things bothering you. When you share with someone who loves you and who is willing to listen to what you have to say, you stop bottling everything in and can experience the positive impact of someone having empathy for what you are going through. This helps you validate and accept your feelings to then look for ways to move on from them intentionally.

If you choose to talk to someone about your stressors, be sure to let them know if you need help with your stressors, or if you are just looking to vent. This way, you receive the exact support you need. Do not be afraid to ask for different opinions or perspectives on what you are going through, too, because you may be able to learn about unique takes on your current problem that you had not thought of before. Sometimes, getting a different perspective on something gives you everything you need to step outside of the stressful position and find understanding and closure in a troubling situation. Then, you will find that you have the energy you need to stop procrastinating and start conquering the important task that can no longer wait to be tackled.

Chapter 6: Your Need For A Motivational Vision

Motivational visions are one of the greatest secrets for success. Professionals in virtually every industry use them to motivate themselves to get things done, especially when they are doing things that they are not incredibly excited about doing. Yes, even the top professionals that you look up to find themselves in situations where something they need to do sucks, and nothing is going to convince them otherwise, not even themselves. Rather than trying to convince yourself that a necessary task does not suck, accept that it does and find a way to motivate yourself anyway. The sooner you get reality and aim to look at it from a different angle, rather than try to force an angle that just isn't working, the sooner you will be able to find a solution that works so you can keep yourself going. Motivational visions are that solution.

The Value Of Motivational Visions

A motivational vision is a vision that allows you to consider the effect of all of the steps you are taking toward generating success in any given area of your life. Rather than fixating on the success that you will experience in any specific circumstance, it seeks to motivate you by allowing you to fixate on the overall success that you are aiming for. This way, you can feel deeply inspired by the vision because it reflects things that you care about. For example, maybe you are exercising because you want to have enough energy to keep up with your children, so rather than visualizing a successful workout, you visualize being able to run around and play with your children in the future.

Developing motivational visions that reflect precisely what you are working toward and that you care about most ensures that your visions actually work. By enticing your emotions and promising a future of everything you want, they enable you to push through any feelings of frustration, boredom, or resistance to accomplish any task that needs to be completed.

Creating A Positive Visualization That Works

For a motivational vision to work, it needs to reflect a form of success that you deeply care about. It should not just be something you are interested in, that would be fun to have, or that you want for frivolous reasons. For example, visualizing having a lot of money because you want to earn status so that people treat you better is a pretty superficial dream that is unlikely to motivate you to do anything. However, visualizing having respect for yourself and accepting consideration from your peers as a bonus is a beautiful motivational vision. You need to be deeply attached to the vision you are carrying, which is precisely why it needs to correspond to one of your deepest and most meaningful core desires.

You also need a visualization that is going to allow you to connect it to your real life. Creating a vision that you cannot believe in or that does not seem realistic to your life is unlikely to motivate you because, despite how entertaining it may be to visualize, it does not seem possible. Therefore it seems pointless to put the energy toward it. A realistic vision is sure to help keep you on track and get you the success you desire.

Designing A Multi-Sensory Experience

Your brain cannot tell the difference between a visualization and a real experience. It can, however, tell the difference between a meaningful memory and a non-meaningful one. Meaningful memories are ones that linger and manifest as full memories, while non-meaningful ones are vague and difficult to put together. For a quick example of what I mean, think back to the most exciting day. What was it like? Can you visualize how it felt, what you saw, what you heard, what you were eating, or what you were smelling? Chances are, if you were to close your eyes, you could transport yourself back into that memory as though you were reliving it right here and now. Now, recall the last time you went to the grocery store. Unless something meaningful happened, chances are you cannot remember what happened. You might be able to place yourself in the grocery store because you go there often enough, but you likely cannot recall that specific trip in great detail. That is because it is not a significant or essential memory.

Turning your motivational vision into a multi-sensory experience ensures that it is implanted in your brain as a meaningful memory, which means you will be able to put yourself in the scene as though you were reliving it. Even though you have not experienced it yet, this is still possible. You can create this type of multi-sensory experience by considering what your vision would be like if you were experiencing it at that moment. What would you see, touch, taste, smell, and hear? Be specific, and try to interact with those aspects of the experience so you can turn them into something real and memorable. Every time you do this, your vision will become even more robust, and it will become even more ingrained in your brain as something natural, easy, and worth the effort.

Tapping Into Visualization For Motivation

Remembering to tap into your motivational visualization is one of the most critical aspects of gaining any value from it. Many experts claim that you should visualize for at least 10 minutes per day if you want it to come true, as it gets you in the right mindset for success, and it allows you to create more for yourself. While this is important and is certainly worth the effort, you should also start practicing tapping into your motivational visualization when you need a boost of motivation. For example, if you have been putting off taking the necessary steps to get into a healthier wellness routine due to procrastination, you could tap into your motivational visualization to help. The next time you schedule a workout session or when it comes time to cook a healthy meal, spend 2-3 minutes visualizing your motivational visualization, then get started. You might even stretch or exercise your body as you do your visualization practice, which will give you a double serving of motivation to get you going!

Developing Your Visualization Over Time

Over time, you may find that your previous visualization is not as relevant as it once was. For example, once you start reaching certain milestones, your desires may change, or you might find that at some point, your previous desires are no longer relevant, and you are inspired by something else. When you feel this happening, allow yourself to develop your vision to resemble something accurate to what you are working toward in the present. This way, your visualization continues to represent something you are passionate about and will continue to offer the motivational energy you need to keep moving forward.

Part 2: Uninstall the Virus

Chapter 7: What It Actually Takes To Stop Procrastinating

The real reason why you cannot stop procrastinating is that you do not yet have the magical keys that will unlock your unique blend of motivation and get you out of the rut you have found yourself in. If you find success in freeing yourself from this cycle, you need to understand yourself more deeply, and you need to start taking small practical steps toward elevating yourself out of the challenges you are presently facing. Once you understand your unique reason behind procrastinating and the specific elements of your procrastination cycle, it will become easier for you to take the necessary action to stop it. That's right: the real reason your efforts have not worked is that, until now, they have been *too generic*.

Why Are YOU Procrastinating?

In part one, we got specific on the reasons as to why people procrastinate, and why they continue procrastinating even after they realize their behavior has become problematic. Now, you need to sit and brainstorm your specific reasoning behind procrastinating, and what has motivated you to continue procrastinating even after realizing that it has become a problematic behavior for you. Refrain from summarizing it as being a form of laziness, because that in and of itself would be real laziness, and it would also be incredibly inaccurate.

If your reflections are not revealing the true reason behind your procrastination, try defining your procrastination cycle first and then reflect on that. Sometimes, pausing and observing what is going on is all you need to identify the exact issues you face. They may not be quite as obvious, which is typical for procrastinators or anyone who engages in any form of self-sabotage. Once you can see the real reason, though, addressing it will become far more manageable.

Define Your Procrastination Cycle

Defining your procrastination cycle takes some time and consistency. You need to start at the beginning by identifying something you want to do, and then following your process as you work toward doing it. For example, let's say you decide you want to run a business, and you have a specific business in mind, such as a blog. As soon as you come up with an idea like this, write the idea down on a piece of paper. Now, keep track of everything you do, or do not do, toward making that come to life. Write down what your plans are, and any scheduled time you have set aside, and write down what happens when it comes time to fulfill those plans or engage in that scheduled activity. Don't just write down your actions, write down the thoughts and feelings you had regarding those actions, too. This way, you have a clear understanding of what is going on with you every time you attempt to pursue something meaningful to you.

If you cannot get past the point of procrastination, or if it seems like your goal is taking far too long for you to act on, you can stop tracking it after about four weeks and start reviewing your cycle from there. Chances are, that is your entire cycle, and the process of actually getting to work and getting anything done is not currently a part of your cycle.

Get Clear About Your Motivation And Rewards

In monitoring your procrastination cycle, you will likely identify your motivation and rewards relatively quickly. Your inspiration drives you to procrastinate, while the reward is what you are gaining from procrastinating. The generic answer to this cycle is that you are motivated to not have to do the work associated with the task you are procrastinating from, and the reward is that when you engage in your distraction, you justify not doing the work.

The real clarity you need to gain here is why you are being motivated not to take action on your desired tasks. Are you bored? Frustrated? Not feeling challenged enough? Uninterested in the possible results? When you begin to understand why you are motivated to behave the way you do, it becomes easier to understand where the reward comes in from the actions you are taking. Through this understanding, you can begin to develop a plan for how you will pivot your actions and eliminate behaviors of procrastination from your life.

Engage In Deep Self-Forgiveness

Before you take any action toward improving your procrastination, you need to decide to engage in deep self-forgiveness. Even a single act of procrastination can lead to unfortunate side effects, which means if you have been procrastinating for a while, you have likely endured many consequences from your actions. These consequences can lead to feelings of disappointment, guilt, jealousy, embarrassment, shame, loss, grief, and many other things caused by you not taking action when you said you would.

Moving these emotions out of the way by practicing self-forgiveness will help you let yourself off the hook to be more patient with yourself as you learn how to do better than you did previously. Not forgiving yourself may lead to you using each future mistake as evidence that you are incapable of change, rather than proof that you can witness these mistakes and use them to help you make changes.

The most effective way to engage in self-forgiveness is to sit and think about all of the unfortunate things you have experienced due to your procrastination. Jot down everything, whether you believe it still bothers you or not, and take a serious look at what you have experienced as a result of your actions. Take a moment to feel through all of the feelings that come with recognizing how much procrastination has cost you, then start working toward reframing everything in your mind using forgiveness and acceptance. Become willing to see how your past actions have hurt you and accept that you didn't know better at the time, which is precisely why you could not break free from the habits you were engaged in. Forgive yourself for the actions you took, and accept that you are unable to change what you have done, but you can start to fix your behavior now, so you are no longer affected in the same way you once were. Realize that you deserve to experience better, and resolve to do everything to ensure that you will do better in the future.

Once you have come to acceptance around what you have already experienced, you also need to commit to forgiving yourself for any mistakes you make in the future. Remember, forgiving yourself does not mean condoning your poor choices or permitting yourself to settle for the mistakes you make it means that you will not let your mistakes serve as evidence that you are incapable of change. Instead, you will use your ability to witness your mistakes as evidence that you can learn from them and make the necessary changes to grow as a person.

Apply The Power Of The Pivot

After you have laid the foundation of forgiveness, you need to plan your path to a resolution using the power of the pivot. The power of the pivot requires you to think back to your motivation and reward and start looking for new, more productive habits you can engage in that fulfill that same motivation by providing you with your desired reward. For example, let's say you have not cleaned your kitchen because it seems like a boring thing to do, and you have no desire to get it done. Instead, you play video games because it is more enjoyable and it entertains you better than doing the dishes would. In this case, you need to find a way to make doing the dishes more entertaining so you can be rewarded with entertainment. Perhaps you make a game out of doing the dishes, you make this the time that you listen to your favorite music or audiobook, or you call your friends while you are doing the dishes so you can catch up with each other. By including a more entertaining element, you eliminate the boredom factor and allow your chores to become more enjoyable.

Pivots may not always make the task at hand delightful. Likely, many of them will still suck, and you will still find yourself considering them to be a boring task no matter what way you look at it, and that's fine. The key is not to change your mind about the task at hand, but to do what you can to make it less sucky so you can motivate yourself to get it done more easily.

Anytime you define a pivot, always look for a pivot that will fulfill the motivation with the same reward using different actions. From your brain's perspective, facilitating this change is far more comfortable than changing from one motivation or reward to an entirely different motivation or reward. This is because, as far as neurology goes, these neural pathways are already defined, and it is easier to adjust existing neural pathways than to attempt to deny existing neural pathways while creating new ones altogether. This simple change is enough to make everything else you do to negate unwanted patterns far easier, whether it be procrastination or anything else you want to change about yourself.

Move Forward With Your New Approach

The follow-through is equally essential to the action you take; you must take action on every decision you make to get the results you desire. Following through is the hardest part of making a change because the steps feel foreign and uncomfortable compared to what you are used to. They are not comfortable, familiar, or so easy that they come like second nature. They require you to think, apply different skills, and work in overdrive to motivate yourself and keep yourself believing that the changes you make are worthy of the efforts you are putting in. At first, it will feel uncomfortable, and everything inside of you will be trying to get you to do it in a safe and familiar way. Still, as you start to see the evidence growing, proving that you are getting better results in this new way, it will become easier.

One of the critical strategies for following through is to make a plan before it is time to put the effort in, and then commit to following that plan no matter what. A significant mistake people make is believing their goal is not working and attempting to adjust it halfway through, when in reality, what they are experiencing is resistance from their psyche, which wants to go back to the "comfortable" way of things. Persevere with your existing plan, unless it genuinely does not work, until you overcome that feeling of having to do things differently. Then, if after a few weeks, you still feel the same way, you can start to make some minor adjustments to get yourself on the right track.

Chapter 8: The Magic Of Accountability

Regardless of how long you have been procrastinating, procrastination deteriorates your relationship with yourself. At the root of your behavior lies negative feelings. The significant side effect of this is the inevitable creation of more negative emotions, which eventually leads to you having a poor relationship with yourself. As you continue procrastinating, you lose trust in yourself, and eventually, you become your own most prominent critic. You become aware of the cycle of declaring you will do, try, or start something only to fail to achieve a said thing. As a result, you feel bad about yourself before you even begin, which leads to you doing nothing.

When you stop believing in yourself, it becomes a lot more challenging to break out of unwanted behaviors and experience more tremendous success in your life. You must learn to repair your relationship with yourself while simultaneously eliminating procrastination behaviors to recover from the struggles you have faced completely.

One way to empower your relationship with yourself and shed your procrastinating behaviors is to hold yourself accountable. Accountability ensures that you remain honest and committed to yourself and others and that you use this energy to drive your actions and, as a by-product, your results. Learning how to embrace accountability in a meaningful way helps you use this as a tool to improve your well-being.

Working With An Accountability Partner

Due to your repeated procrastination, it may seem impossible to hold yourself accountable because you have become so used to letting yourself down. You know that no matter what you say or what you do, it seems like you will always procrastinate because you have learned how to reason with and justify your behaviors. When holding yourself accountable is not good enough, it can help work with an accountability partner who can support you with achieving your goals.

An accountability partner should be someone that you value and who has an opinion that you cherish. They should also be invested in what you wish to do so that they care enough to motivate you and hold you accountable. If your accountability partner does not care enough about what you are doing, they may become enablers rather than accountability buddies, which means they begin to enable you to justify why you are not taking action on the things you care about. Enablers may make you feel good in those moments when you are running away from the negative feelings, but in the long run, you realize that they have not helped in any way, and you are still stuck at square one.

An accountability partner who cares and is invested in your results will motivate you to stay on track and inspire you to work through any hardships you face. If you begin to procrastinate, they will lovingly guide you back on track by calling you out on your actions and helping you reason yourself into making changes, rather than justify your inaction.

The right accountability partner will be someone that you do not want to let down or that you want to impress, as this means the dynamic of your relationship will automatically have you trying harder to overcome your procrastination tendencies. Practically, you will feel worse about letting them down than you would about the actions you have to take, which means it becomes easier to motivate yourself into action. As you work toward impressing your accountability partner through your efforts, you also need to work toward impressing yourself and rebuilding your sense of trust and respect within yourself. This way, going forward, you can hold yourself accountable and motivate yourself to reach your fullest potential. While you may always prefer to work with an accountability partner on your more extensive projects, it is valuable to rely on yourself as your accountability partner, too. This will do wonders for your relationship with yourself and your ability to motivate yourself to get things done. A great way to find an accountability partner is to use an online group such as www.getmotivatedbuddies.com. You could also hire a life coach or take a group program relevant to your goal where you can meet people that have the same desires you do.

Taking Ownership For All Aspects Of Yourself

Justifying procrastination because you believe your current problems would be better solved by your future self is a heinous way to break free of your unwanted cycles. If you think that your future self would be better suited to a specific obligation, yet you take no action in the present to get yourself there, you are procrastinating and outright lying to yourself. First, you are overlooking the very fact that you have not taken any action to prepare your future self for the desired commitment. Second, you are assuming that your future self will care about your present desires as much as your current self does. Both of these set you up for failure. Further, they are both routes toward a loss that *you* will endure, regardless of how you get there.

Snap yourself back into reality by realizing that your current self is a reflection of your future self. The actions you take today are the actions you will likely take tomorrow. If today, you are making excuses to put it off and deciding that other things are more important, you will probably do the same thing tomorrow. If, however, you take a moment to take action toward something you desire today, it is likely you will retake action tomorrow. This is why it is incredibly vital that you start taking action on your desires right away, even if that action seems insignificant toward your final goal. For example, if you desire to lose weight, it may seem trivial to sign up for a gym membership and not go on day 1, but you took action toward going. The next day, you can use that same energy to take action on getting yourself there, then you can take action on getting yourself there again the next day. If you want to see a change in your future, you have to start making a change today. Waiting until the future to make changes is a great way to ensure growth never happens because you are setting your future self up for the same failure you have endured today.

If you want to hold yourself accountable, take responsibility for your future self by taking action toward creating a better future *today*. Do at least one thing to terminate your procrastination tendencies today, and take great pride in the results you make even if they seem small. Continue doing this every single day, as you create a healthier future for yourself starting today. If you genuinely want to hold yourself accountable and use your future self to your advantage, *you must start today*. The future is now!

Improving Your Relationship With You

Lacking a positive relationship with yourself for any period can make it challenging to envision cheerful endings for your future self. This effectively ties in with taking ownership of all aspects of yourself by becoming aware of the fact that, even if you genuinely want to believe that your future self will do better, if you do not particularly like yourself right now, then making any changes will be challenging. Think about it as though you were considering a relationship with someone else for a moment. If you started a relationship with a new friend, yet you did not like them because they tend to treat you poorly by not valuing you and the things you care about, it would be hard to want to imagine great things for their future. You likely wouldn't think about them at all, let alone envisioning a positive future for them. The same goes for yourself. If you are not valuing yourself and the things you care about, valuing your future self and taking necessary steps toward your desired goals will be far more challenging. Begin loving your future self right now by taking action on what matters to you.

Although your end-goal is to bust through procrastination, it can help to start with insignificant goals when it comes to rebuilding trust in yourself and developing a greater sense of self-respect. For example, rather than committing to starting a new company, commit to dressing well every day or eating a healthy dinner every day. These are far smaller goals, yet they are still significant in how you feel about yourself and how you take care of yourself. Once you begin to see that you have the motivation required to take action on these small goals, you will start trusting in yourself again, and as your trust grows, so will your sense of self-respect. From there, you can continue setting larger goals and doing everything required of you to meet them, as your trust in yourself continues to evolve and expand over time. Before you know it, you will be building your desired future self through today's actions and setting yourself up for success with any future goals you might have for yourself.

Holding Yourself Accountable In An Effective Way

Effectively holding yourself accountable means to hold yourself responsible in a way that results in you getting things done. Ineffective accountability within yourself leads to you not creating the results you desire, and therefore struggling to experience a positive outcome. Ultimately, inadequate accountability just leads to more procrastination.

Effective accountability is achieved by holding yourself accountable to things you genuinely know you can achieve so that your words and your actions begin to align. As these align, you find yourself creating a more profound sense of trust within yourself, and therefore a more vital ability to believe in yourself and achieve bigger and bigger goals over time without procrastinating along the way.

You can create goals for yourself by using the S.M.A.R.T. goal planning method. The S.M.A.R.T. goal planning method helps you define clear goals with your present level of trust and accountability and can be elevated to match your growing abilities. In other words, the less you procrastinate, the more complex your goals can become. By following this system, you make the path to achieving your goals as pain-free as possible by clearly defining it, and you make it easier to hold yourself accountable to that path, so you are less likely to procrastinate.

To make S.M.A.R.T. goals for yourself, they need to be specific, measurable, accountable, realistic, and time. Precisely defining your goal ensures that you know exactly what you are working toward, which makes it easy for you to turn that into a measurable goal through milestones. Accountability ensures that you know who you are accountable to and how you can perform your accountability check-ins as you work toward each milestone and the goal as a whole. Realistic goals ensure that you are understanding of your current level of ability, which means accounting for your likelihood of procrastinating. For example, if you know that you are procrastinating so bad that you are unlikely even to do your chores, starting with your tasks may be a more realistic starting point than deciding to launch into a new career or start a new business. Lastly, you need to have a timeline attached to your goals, so you know when you want to meet them by. This helps you have something to hold yourself accountable against. It is important that you create reasonable timelines, meaning you have plenty of time to achieve those tasks but not so much time that it becomes easier to procrastinate in the process. Your timelines should be somewhat challenging to motivate you to get into action, but not unrealistic. As you develop your S.M.A.R.T. goals, be absolutely sure to follow through with them, too, so you can build your sense of trust and respect in yourself, effectively increasing your ability to hold yourself accountable on larger goals later on.

Chapter 9: Creating Procrastination-Proof Deadlines and Schedules

Procrastination-proof deadlines and schedules cater to the fact that, while time management is not the root problem nor the main answer to procrastination, it is important to the task completion process. Knowing how to create procrastination-proof deadlines and schedules ensures that as you are working on improving your procrastination tendencies, you are also experiencing immediate relief from your behaviors. This way, you experience rapid change, and you change the very foundations of your behaviors at the same time, so you gain long-term relief from procrastination.

There are several steps you can take when building your schedule to ensure that you are unlikely to procrastinate and more likely to get things done. Many of these behaviors rely less on the practice of creating a solid schedule and more on the practice of creating a schedule that nurtures your need to feel good. When you start to associate feeling good with completing the tasks on your to-do list, you begin to find yourself experiencing greater levels of freedom from procrastination. Over time, getting into action and completing your tasks feels better than procrastinating, which means you are far less likely to revert to procrastination. If you do, you can feel confident that you have the very skills you need to ditch procrastination and return to a more positive and productive system all over again, anytime you need to.

Breaking Larger Tasks Down

Staring at a schedule full of large, intimidating tasks is bound to stir up some negative feelings in virtually anyone that looks at it. You may begin to feel overwhelmed by the amount of energy it will take, resentful toward the burden of your workload, frustrated with your lack of personal time or time for things you enjoy, or otherwise negative toward your schedule. When you start to look at your schedule and feel annoyed with the seemingly larger tasks, it is time to slow down and break those larger tasks down into smaller, more manageable tasks.

Breaking larger tasks down into smaller tasks means you can easily pop those smaller tasks on your schedule without completely dominating your schedule for anyone given area of your life. For example, let's say your children need you to bake a dozen cupcakes for their upcoming class party. Perhaps it would take you two and a half hours to go shopping for the supplies, come home, make the cupcakes, decorate them, and get them carefully delivered to your children's school. Two and a half hours to bake those cupcakes sounds like a major burden, but when you break it down into shopping, baking, decorating, and delivering, it becomes a lot easier. Now, you might realize that you can easily track the shopping part onto your regular grocery trip, which adds maybe 5 minutes to your schedule. Then, you set aside an hour and a half to bake and decorate the cupcakes. If you ask for your children's help, this can be family time, as well, so you are doing something necessary and something you genuinely enjoy. Then, you can deliver the cupcakes when you drop the kids off at school one morning. Breaking the task down in this way makes it far easier to manage, and therefore you are much less likely to have negative associations with it.

Prioritizing Your Tasks

The tasks on your schedule are all important; otherwise, they would not be on your schedule. However, you still need to prioritize your tasks to ensure they are being done at a reasonable time and that they are fulfilling your needs along the way. Prioritizing your tasks will ensure they are completed on time and that they are done during a time when you are actually interested in prioritizing your tasks, and not just doing them because you have to.

For example, let's say next week you have a huge work project to do, you want to spend time with your family, with your spouse, and with yourself. You also have a lunch date planned with a friend you have not seen in some time, and you attend yoga every Tuesday and Thursday morning. You need to prioritize your schedule to ensure that all these things are accomplished at a reasonable time. You could start by adding the scheduled activities to your calendar, as these already have times and dates associated with them. Ensure that things like your work project are worked on during working hours, so you are not left having to work on it outside of working hours, for example. Once the scheduled activities are added, you can look at the remaining time on your calendar and decide which types of activities would be best suited to each area of your remaining time. This way, your schedule makes sense and has properly prioritized everything that is important to you in a non-overwhelming manner.

The Climax Approach To Scheduling

As you break tasks down and prioritize them into your schedule, it can be helpful to follow the climax approach to scheduling your time. The climax approach relies on the climax theory derived from storytelling. When you write a story, you start off with important information that is interesting but not necessarily the most important. As you continue writing, you reach the climax, which includes the most important and interesting part of your story. After the climax, you dwindle back down to a less important and interesting bit of information. This is relevant to procrastination because it means you can time your tasks in a way that makes them easy to do since they follow your natural energy pattern.

For example, let's say you need to clean your garage before winter because you want to be able to store your car in there, rather than keeping it outside in the snow. You might break the process down into the following tasks: remove clutter, empty boxes, donate or sell unwanted items, throw away the trash, organize remaining items, sweep, pull the car in. To turn these tasks into a climax approach, you would start with simple, low-impact tasks like moving all of the clutter out of the way by organizing it into four piles: donate, sell, trash, and keep. Then, you would empty the boxes into those piles, too. Next, you would take the climax tasks of actually donating, throwing away, and selling all the unwanted items, and of organizing the remaining items. Then, you would follow less intense tasks like sweeping and pulling the car into the garage. By doing this, you allow your momentum to grow, use the peak of that energy to do the hardest tasks, and then commit to doing easier things after the largest tasks are done. This way, you work with your natural energy and attention span and effectively get everything done in the process.

Turning Your Schedule Into A Checklist

There is an incredible amount of joy that people gain from being able to check things off of a "to do list". Placing a check next to a completed activity is like receiving a reward for a job well done, and it behaves exactly like that in your mind. When you check something off your to-do list, you experience a small rush of dopamine in your brain that rewards you for completing that task. This creates positive emotions around your checklist and makes you far more likely to actually want to complete tasks on your to-do list because you know it feels good to do it.

When you create your schedule, physically write everything down onto your schedule and give yourself room to check everything off of it on a daily basis. Then, commit to placing those checkmarks every single day. The positive association will continue to grow, and you will find yourself feeling more motivated to get things done, and less motivated to sit around and procrastinate because you are digging straight into the root cause of procrastination itself.

Being Compassionate With Your Schedule

Building an overwhelming, intimidating, or unrealistic schedule is a form of self-abuse. It guarantees that you will feel negative associations with your schedule and that you will be less likely to actually follow through on the schedule and get things done. As you build your schedule, do not just focus on being the most productive you can be; focus on creating a schedule that is also enjoyable for you to follow. When you can genuinely look forward to your schedule because you have included plenty of time for productivity and for fun and relaxation, it becomes far easier to feel positive when looking at your schedule. This also makes it easier to motivate yourself to get the less enjoyable portions of your schedule done because you know you have plenty of wonderful things to look forward to once those tasks are completed.

Self-Motivating Routines To Get You Going

Self-motivating routines are an excellent practice to use when you want to create a stronger sense of positive energy around your schedule. These routines are designed to make you feel good about the task that needs to be done, either by making the task sound more enjoyable or by emphasizing the joy you will feel when the task is complete. You can use these routines to build your mental, emotional, and physical energy, while also using them to help you recognize the value of the task you are completing. Through this, you can essentially give yourself the momentum you need to get through any task on your schedule, no matter how big or small it may be.

Self-motivating routines can be simple pep talks, or they can be more intense practices that really get your blood pumping. Many business professionals, such as Tony Robbins, use a quick physical exercise routine that gets their blood pumping. This routine is usually just enough to get them moving, but not enough to cause them to sweat, as they do not want to look unpleasant when they walk into important meetings. A great routine would be to jump up and down a couple of times and then run on the spot, or to stretch your body out from your head all the way to your toes. As you do, repeat a positive mantra to yourself so you can pump up your mind and emotions, too. Then, use that energy to get started on your next task. After you have completed the task, reward yourself, and celebrate yourself as much as possible, as this will reinforce your self-motivational efforts.

Chapter 10: Getting Resilient With Discomfort

Discomfort is an inevitable part of life. When it comes to procrastination, discomfort is exactly what you are trying to avoid, as you move back and forth between trying to avoid the negative feelings associated with doing the task, and later the negative feelings of realizing it's not yet complete. It is often said that change happens when the pain of staying the same becomes greater than the pain of change. When there is an underlying negative emotion associated with the task you are avoiding, you are likely going to procrastinate until the pain and pressure of not getting the task done are greater than the discomfort of the task itself.

Building awareness and understanding around the discomfort you experience when trying to perform certain tasks can help you mitigate the negative feelings and minimize the tendency to procrastinate. Building a stronger mindset and a more positive and motivating approach is very effective in countering procrastination in the long run; however, sometimes, you just have to swallow the bitter pill and just get on with it.

Have you ever done something that was uncomfortable, something you didn't feel like doing at the time? Maybe you were in a situation where you seemingly had no choice but to go ahead and do it, even though you were paralyzed with fear. After getting over your discomfort and getting it done, remember how proud you felt. It is a false assumption that we have to always feel comfortable or feel motivated to get started with something. In fact, you don't have to feel anything to get started with something. You don't have to feel excited to wash the dishes, nor let the feeling of disgust towards the task stop you. It is possible to get things done despite the way we feel about them. Next time you find yourself procrastinating because you don't feel like doing the task at hand, remind yourself that you don't have to feel like doing it and just get started. Get started in spite of not feeling like it, just to prove to your subconscious mind that you can. This approach to dealing with discomfort will go a long way in helping you overcome procrastination by building your resiliency and helping you create the courage to complete things you do not necessarily enjoy.

Increasingly Delaying Your Gratification

Delaying gratification is like training yourself to wait longer and longer for the satisfaction you seek, while also gradually transitioning away from sources of instant gratification in favor of more satisfying sources of gratification. You want to put space between yourself and mindless or pointless sources of gratification, such as scrolling social media, watching irrelevant videos, video gaming, or otherwise mindlessly wasting your time. While all of these activities can be enjoyed in moderation, procrastinators tend to use them as a way to distract themselves and create an instant sense of fulfillment, rather than as an intentional way to connect with others or be entertained.

Each time you find yourself feeling urged to engage in the form of instant gratification, stop and breathe for a few moments. Let yourself focus on the task at hand longer each time, until eventually, it is easy for you to breathe through the urge and ignore it entirely. Reward yourself later with a few moments of that very same reward, in moderation, of course. For example, if you manage to wait an extra 20 minutes before scrolling social media, give yourself 3-5 minutes to scroll it before resuming your original task or moving onto your next task. This way, you receive that reward, and you also experience a sense of fulfillment from having completed the important task you were focusing on, too.

Being Mindful Of Your Instant Gratification Urges

Being mindful about your instant gratification urges is a great way to delay your gratification, as well. When you experience an urge to engage in some form of instant gratification, ask yourself where the urge is coming from, what your real desire is, and why you are experiencing this particular urge. These questions help you become more mindful of the urge itself, which allows you to navigate the urge intentionally. Rather than mindlessly giving in and justifying it as being "no big deal," you can become aware of the real desire behind your urge and look for ways to use that urge to motivate you rather than distract you. For example, if you were looking for the chance to quickly increase the level of excitement you were gaining out of your time, rather than giving in to the distraction, you could find a way to make your current task more exciting. Perhaps you start listening to some music as you work on it, creating a hyper-specific checklist for the next 5-10 things you need to do, and excitedly checking each one-off, or bragging to yourself about how much you have done so far. This mindful approach is an excellent way to bring your mind back to the task at hand so you can refrain from being distracted, and instead, get your job done.

Rewarding Yourself For Doing It The Right Way

Anytime you engage in a task and do not succumb to procrastination, you should reward yourself for that success. Celebrate yourself, talk yourself up in your mind, give yourself a few minutes of something pleasurable to do, and otherwise reward yourself for a job well done. Overcoming procrastination is easiest when you feel a rush of positive emotion every time you create your desired results since it is negative emotions that you are trying to escape. By rewarding yourself and giving yourself positive reinforcement for everything you have accomplished, you are effectively transitioning yourself away from procrastination and into a state of motivation.

Making A Conscious Decision And Commitment To "You "

Lastly, if you find yourself truly struggling with becoming resilient toward discomfort so you can make stronger choices for yourself, you need to make a conscious decision to commit to yourself. You must become willing to commit more deeply and completely than you ever have in your entire life. You need to decide that you can and will keep working on yourself, continuously, because you deserve the better things in life that come from a deep commitment to self-improvement. You may be wondering if I have a secret or a tidbit I can offer you that will help you turn your commitment into an easy, no-brainer that is effortless for you to follow through on. I have to tell you the truth; there is no secret or tidbit. You need to be willing to hold yourself up to a higher standard. You can decide to love and respect yourself more and consequently treat yourself and your potential with more reverence. For better or worse, you need to accept the experiences that come with commitments and be willing to work through them. Be mindful about what this commitment means to you, and ready to continually re-commit anytime you find yourself faltering or struggling. The more you get into the habit of choosing to uphold your commitment, the easier and more natural it will become.

Chapter 11: Positivity Is Overrated, Get Realistic Instead

Positivity has immense power over your success. Yes, on one hand, you need to talk in a positive manner and build a positive, thriving relationship with yourself. Kind, compassionate, and empowering self-talk goes a long way toward improving your sense of wellbeing and your overall ability to achieve your desires. However, positivity is not the only place you need to look when it comes to overcoming behaviors such as procrastination.

As humans, we have two different ways that we are motivated. You can either be motivated by the fear of pain or the desire for pleasure. The majority of humans are primarily motivated by the fear of pain, despite the fact that they long for pleasure. This means that while they do desire pleasure, this desire in and of itself is not always strong enough to motivate them into action (especially if they already feel comfortable - the promise of more comfort is not motivating enough for them to leave their current comfort zone), while the fear of pain is often the true motivating factor behind most action.

As of right now, you are using your fear of pain to motivate you *not* to take action. While positivity will help you feel better, it is unlikely to be enough to motivate you to take significant action because it is simply not strong enough to do so. Rather than relying exclusively on positivity, you need to discover how to use your fear of pain to your advantage so that it can motivate you to get into action. This is effectively achieved using mindset skills and a change in perspective.

Positivity VS. Optimism And How They Affect Procrastination

You cannot override your negative thoughts and feelings with positive ones, despite how much you may try. It is perfectly reasonable to be realistic about the things you do not enjoy in life, and it is a large waste of energy to attempt to pretend you enjoy the things you don't. At the end of the day, if something sucks to do, it's going to suck to do regardless of how you try to change your mind around it. Rather than wasting energy on changing your mind into something more positive, it is better to focus on optimism. Optimism states that while something might be crummy to do at the moment, the outcome is desirable and, therefore, worth it. You exert far less energy cultivating this mindset and, in the process, give yourself far more energy to achieve other things in life.

Beyond that, negative emotions can be highly motivating. Anger, for example, can drive you to accomplish many things. Think about it, the last time you got angry with someone, it eventually reached a point where you had to say something about it, and you likely did not back down until the enraging circumstances changed. You had finally become angry enough that you would not stop until you reached your goal. The same can be achieved in other situations, too. For example, if you become angry enough with your current job, you might use that anger to finally start your own company, effectively removing you from the unwanted situation. Anger is a powerful emotion that always seeks release, often through physical action. While anger is not a good long-term motivational strategy, it can be used in the heat of the moment when you need it.

Becoming Realistic About Your Abilities

Becoming more realistic about what you can and cannot do is an excellent way to create space for you to get the job done. The reality is, you are going to be awful at some things. With certain activities, you will get better over time, and with others, you won't. Accepting your abilities as they are right now is a better way to get yourself into action because you are not attempting to pretend that you are capable of doing more than you can reasonably do. When you refuse to lie to yourself to pump yourself up, you build trust in yourself. You also allow yourself to focus on getting the job done, rather than pretending you're having fun with the job in the first place.

Here is where it is especially beneficial to zoom out on your current activities and get a larger perspective on everything going on. Yes, it might suck to have to do this particular task; however, the benefits you gain from this task is that it will be done and you can reap the rewards of its completion.

Anytime you find you dislike a task that you need to complete, immediately start focusing on the benefits of getting it done. Then, commit to taking just five minutes to get started on that particular task. After you get the first five minutes done, you will likely develop enough momentum to keep you going until you get the current task done. Often, when you are physically engaged in a task, it sucks less than you thought it would. Things tend to suck more in your mind when you anticipate having to do a task than when you are actually doing them, which is why focusing on the long term results and committing to just a short effort, to begin with, can be so beneficial.

Holding Space For Reality

A major drawback of chronic positive thinking that many people do not realize to be so troublesome is that, if you always try to achieve everything with positive thinking, you will be lying to yourself a lot. In those lies, you will find yourself experiencing a lack of trust in yourself, which, as you know, worsens your tendency to procrastinate. The reality is, some things are going to suck. Sometimes, parts of a task, or even an entire task itself, is not going to be enjoyable. No matter how you look at it, there is no way to see or find positivity or joy in that task. For me, that task is cleaning the bathroom. *I hate it.* No matter how I look at it, scrubbing the toilet and the shower and the sink is a sucky chore. *But it has to be done.* I can either procrastinate and then feel ashamed when people come over and see my atrociously dirty bathroom; I can try to convince myself it is a positive thing and become annoyed with myself because I can't stand it, or I can accept it for being sucky. Rather than feel ashamed or annoyed, I would rather accept that it is not a chore I enjoy doing and instead look at the reality of it being a terrible chore to have to do.

Even when we look at things through realistic eyes, we can continue to find some level of optimism to keep us going. With the bathroom, for example, I cannot find any optimism in the chore itself. However, I can find optimism in the results I gain from the chore, which is knowing I have a clean bathroom to use, and that I will not feel ashamed if people come over and use my bathroom. You can likely find similar levels of optimism in your crummy situations to convince you that while, yes, the task does suck, there is still value to getting it done. This way, you can be honest with yourself and continue anyway without the frustration of procrastination creeping in and leading to unwanted consequences later on.

Chapter 12: Don't Waste Your Willpower

Willpower is a commonly discussed topic that refers to a level of energy that one has, which can be exerted to achieve a certain goal. In layman's terms, willpower is that burst of energy you feel that motivates you to either do or not do something. For example, if you want to start going to the gym to work out four times a week, you might use willpower to motivate you to get to the gym and start your workout.

While willpower is indeed a powerful energy, it is not everything that people think it is. Many people believe that willpower, and willpower alone, is responsible for your ability to make life changes, but research has proven that this is not the case. This is why, if you have been blaming a lack of willpower for your inability to overcome procrastination or to help you "stop being so lazy," you have been relying on the wrong information. Willpower will certainly help you get out of these behaviors but it, alone, is not enough to get you where you need to go. You must learn how to move beyond willpower and into a far greater level of behavioral change and motivation if you will successfully change your ways and embody a permanent level of change.

Willpower Is A Limited Resource

The reason why willpower alone is not strong enough to motivate lasting change is that willpower is a limited resource. Willpower provides you with momentary energy to make a preferred decision, and then, just like that, the energy is gone. Willpower feeds on the novelty of a situation, which means any time you are trying something new and different, willpower will be at its strongest. When you move beyond the novelty of something, willpower begins to dwindle because the excitement is not there to feed your willpower the energy it needs to motivate you into action. This is why willpower seems strong and effective for the first few days, or even weeks, of a new habit, and then it dwindles, and you revert to your old ways.

Being aware of the reality of what willpower is means you can use it in a specific and intentional manner, and you can quickly move past willpower and into stronger levels of motivation and change as willpower begins to naturally fade. Although willpower is a limited resource, it is also a powerful resource and can certainly be used to help you create change in your life. You can fuel your willpower by building up your excitement around a new change you are making in your life. As you build this excitement, focus on doing so in a way that encourages your energy to grow around the change itself, as well as in a way that allows you to plan for how you will proceed after willpower is depleted.

The more excitement you have going into a new situation, the more likely you will be to effectively rely on willpower for the first several days or even weeks of that new change. Then, you can begin to rely on other more long-lasting motivations such as habits and permanent lifestyle changes to keep you going, as these will be far more sustainable than willpower alone.

Use Willpower To Build Your Habits

The most effective way to use willpower and create sustainable, life-long change is to use willpower to build new habits. This is where most people make a major mistake and misuse willpower, which leads back to them, not creating the lasting change they wanted, and it damages their self-esteem and self-confidence in the meantime. The more you fail to make a permanent change in your life, such as by terminating your procrastination tendencies once and for all, the less confident you feel in your ability to ever make such a change. Fortunately, that can be changed once you have the right information in your possession.

By using willpower to build your habits, you use this powerful yet limited resource to help you lay the foundation for permanent lifestyle changes based on the new habits you are creating. This way, even long after willpower is depleted, your brain has been wired for these new habits and, therefore, naturally motivates you to fulfill them because your brain is addicted to habits and loves doing things in a habitual manner. A great example of using willpower to motivate a habit that motivates change would be to use willpower to motivate yourself to get your gym shoes on, grab your gym back, and head out the door every morning. This way, rather than motivating yourself to go to the gym, you are motivating yourself to get into the habit of leaving for the gym. Once willpower runs out, you will be in the habit of putting on your gym shoes, grabbing your bag, and leaving. From there, you simply have to follow the habit, which is easy to do because your brain wants to experience the reward portion of fulfilling one of your habits.

Leverage Your Habits To Build Your Success Rates

Your success rates are exceptionally low when you procrastinate on a regular basis. Chances are, you follow through and achieve extremely few of the things you say you want to do, and this is largely based on poor habits. Leveraging healthy habits to build your success rates means you gain the ability to achieve far more of the things you say you will do. It works by understanding which habits will motivate success, and giving everything you have to build these habits.

As you break out of procrastination, there are two types of habits to form that will help break free from procrastination and find greater success in jumping into action. The first set of habits are those related specifically to procrastinating behaviors, while the second set is related to the areas of your life where you tend to procrastinate the most.

For habits relating to your procrastinating behaviors, develop stronger habits that enable you to eliminate distractions and get into action anytime you witness procrastination starts. This is easiest achieved by recognizing which distractions are affecting you worst, and which habits are encouraging you to engage in those distractions in the first place. By creating counter habits, you effectively prevent yourself from engaging in those habits before they even begin, making it much easier to avoid procrastination altogether. For example, let's say your phone is your biggest distraction, and you tend to pull your phone out anytime you do not want to be doing anything else. You can combat this by getting into the habit of putting your phone somewhere far away from you and leaving it there unless you are intentionally checking it for something.

The second type of habit that you need to have, targets specific scenarios where you are likely to procrastinate. For example, if you tend to procrastinate when it comes to eating healthy, taking action on your career, or making progress toward your personal goals, you need to develop habits in these specific areas of your life. Presently, your habits are not enabling you to experience success in these areas of your life, so discovering healthier, more effective habits ensure you get the results you desire. For example, let's say no matter how you try to get yourself to go to the gym, you never follow through. Perhaps you have tried starting a membership, hiring a personal trainer, buying books, following podcasts that are meant to build motivation, and adjusting the time of day that you go to the gym. Maybe you have bought all the clothes that you want to work out in, and you feel you have everything aligned, and when it comes to everything about going to the gym, you are great at it, except for *actually getting there*. For some reason, you can never seem to get yourself through the door, so you can start your workout. There is always an excuse that seems more significant than your desire to get fit, so it never happens. In this case, you need healthier habits around getting yourself to the gym so you can exercise regularly. A great set of habits to combat this would be to get into the habit of getting your shoes on at your designated gym time, driving to the gym, and getting in the front door. Once you are in the front door, the only logical thing to do is work out, so leave that part aside and focus on getting yourself in the door for starters. All other exercise-related habits can be developed *after* you get into the habit of starting your workout.

When you develop the right habits for your success, getting the results you desire becomes far easier. Procrastination is far less problematic when you have habitual routines built-in to your brain that encourage you to get started and get your job done.

Never Try To Break Or Make Habits

While we are on the topic of habit creation, let's discuss the number one way to fail when it comes to creating new habits. Since habits will be your golden ticket to ending procrastination for good, you need to know how habits work and what must be done for habits to be eliminated or created in your life. This way, you can effectively break the habit of procrastinating and get into the habit of actually getting things done!

The number one thing that sabotages your ability to make or break habits is actually *trying* to make or break habits. To better understand this, you first need to understand what is going on in your brain when you create and engage in habitual behavior. Your habits are created through something known as a habit loop, and, unsurprisingly, your habit loop is similar to a cycle of procrastination. The habit starts with a trigger, moves into a learned behavior, and ends with a reward. The chosen behavior is one that has proven to create the desired reward time and again. A great example of this would be every time you turn on the TV and binge-watch your favorite show, rather than get your work done. At that moment, you are craving a feel-good rush of dopamine, and your work has proven to be ineffective in creating that rush for you. Your favorite show, however, offers it. The trigger: you needing to complete a specific work-related task. The activity: procrastinating by watching TV instead of getting the work done. The reward: a dopamine rush created through instant gratification. Your brain thinks you are succeeding because it feels good and you have avoided expending energy on a task that made you feel "not so good" so, next time you're in that same situation, your brain is going to encourage the same behavioral response - easy like that, a habit is born.

When you try to make or break a habit, you fail to understand that your brain has already created millions of habits that are designed to fulfill specific rewards. You partake in those habits every single day, and every time without fail, you experience the specific reward that your brain is looking for. By trying to break a habit, you remove your ability to experience a specific reward that your brain is looking for. By trying to make a brand new habit, you attempt to force your brain to experience a new reward that it was not actually looking for, and so it does not register the reward, or it looks for a similar reward that it already knows how to get more easily. Thus, you fail.

If you want to create new habits or break unwanted habits, you need to stop trying to take a from-scratch approach and start working with your brain in a way that allows you to actually get your desired results. That is, you need to start embracing the art of shifting or pivoting your habits, as this means you are already working with a developed habit-loop, and your brain is already through the hard part of habit creation. When you do this, you work with your brain to eliminate the habit of procrastination, which means your brain will *want* to help you stop that particular habit, and not just because your logical mind is forcing it to, either.

The Creation Of New Habits Lies In The Pivot

"Old habits die hard" - we all have heard the old expression. But why is that?

When a particular behavior is repeated enough times, our brain forms a sort of shortcut that allows it to conserve energy and make it easier to execute that behavior subsequently. That is how we learn, and our brain is learning all the time, even when we think we're doing nothing important, like watching TV.

Once the shortcut has been established, it is hard to remove. It's like riding a bicycle - once you learn how to do it, you never forget it. The same goes for our habits.

This is where the power of the pivot comes in - instead of fighting an old habit, we overwrite it with a new one.

The creation of new habits, and the destruction of old habits, lies in the pivot. To pivot your habit means that you take an existing habit and shift it so that you achieve the same reward that is fulfilled following the same trigger, but it is accomplished in a new way. To make this as clear as possible, let's quickly review the habit loop: trigger, behavior, reward, repeat. When you pivot, the trigger, reward, and repeat portion of the loop remain the same. The only thing that changes is the behavior. In this case, you will be changing the behavior related to procrastination, but you will continue to receive the same reward that has been motivating you to procrastinate in the first place.

To create this shift, you first need to take a look at your procrastination cycle and understand how it fits into the habit loop. You may need to do this for each individual area of your life where you are procrastinating, particularly if you realize that you have been procrastinating for different reasons in each area of your life.

To witness the procrastination cycle against the habit loop, you will need to stop and be mindful of the process anytime you realize you have been procrastinating. Ideally, you should observe it at least 3-5 times before doing anything to change it, as this will help you develop a stronger understanding of why it happens and how you can fix it. Look to understand what triggered the procrastination, what specific behaviors were involved in you procrastinating, what the reward in that exact moment felt like, and what was motivating you to repeat this behavior. Know that with procrastination, the reward may not be anything significant or even obvious. It may be something as simple as "I avoided performing a task that seemed tedious and boring at the time - I conserved energy ."

As soon as you have understood the cycle, you need to start looking for new behaviors that will provide the same reward. This part takes some planning, as you have to figure out which new behavior will stop you from procrastinating while still fulfilling that same reward.

For example, people who are trying to eat healthier but have a habit of snacking might replace unhealthy snacks like chips, cookies, etc. with healthier ones such as dried fruit, nuts, and seeds, instead of trying to stop snacking altogether. Or people who have gone off smoking cigarettes by using vapor based e-devices.

I have a habit that feeds my procrastination. Whenever I sit down at my computer to do some work, the first thing I will do is check my email and social media. I would tell myself that it won't take more than 15 minutes, but an hour later, I find myself watching tech reviews on YouTube, wondering how I ended up there.

I realized that I couldn't avoid the trigger (sitting down at my computer), so I changed my response to it. Now, when I boot up my computer, I will stand up (this disrupts my usual pattern) and do a nice long stretch, then close my eyes and visualize the work I am about to do and why it is important, what are the long term benefits. This little routine takes only a minute or two, provides a similar reward by delaying the work for just a bit, feels good, and at the end of it, I find it much easier to get straight to work, avoiding my usual response of checking email first. Another thing I like to do is launch my music for work playlist first thing after booting up the computer - music helps me focus.

So long as the initial reward is being fulfilled, you will have a much easier time making this pivot.

Once you have figured out your new behavior shift, you will need to use willpower to motivate you to make that shift the first several times. Eventually, your willpower will begin to fade, but your brain will realize that this new behavior achieves the same results; therefore, it has an easier time motivating you to complete this new behavior.

This way of pivoting more productive behavior around your old habits can be a very powerful tool in your anti-procrastination toolbox and also help you with building new, more desirable habits in general.

Chapter 13: Leverage Your Power Hour

Have you ever wondered how some people are able to wake up, get started with their day, and achieve massive success on a daily basis? Many have sought to understand what sets these successful individuals apart from everyone else, but the gist of it is simple. The success achieved by these individuals is not achieved by having a four-leaf clover in their pocket, or the gift of luck bestowed upon them. It is achieved by understanding that there is a sweet spot in their day where, if they do everything right, they can give themselves the momentum they need to create success for the rest of the day. If you learn how to tap into this sweet spot yourself, you can give yourself the momentum you need to keep your day going, which will effectively squeeze out any chance you might have had to start procrastinating throughout the day.

What Is A Power Hour?

A power hour is better recognized as being a specific time during the morning, where you have the ability to completely set the tone for your entire day. This also happens to be the time of day where you have the highest level of willpower for that day, as well as a significant amount of focus to apply toward your goals. Using your "power hour" to do the most important or challenging tasks of your day ensures they are completed, as it ensures you are likely to actually take action. Further, they can motivate you to keep going and get even more done that day.

Whatever you do during this hour will determine how successful the rest of your day is because it wires your brain for the day ahead. If you use this power hour for sitting around, drink coffee, and resist getting ready for the day, the rest of your day will seem as though you have no energy and will be full of resistance and an effort to avoid getting anything done. If, however, you use this power hour to get up and get yourself going, you will develop a positive momentum that keeps you going for the rest of the day.

Your power hour is usually marked by the first hour that you are awake. What you do immediately upon opening your eyes defines your day. Most people, especially those who have a hard time with procrastination, will find themselves using this time to scroll their phone, lay in bed as long as they can, and wait until the last possible minute to get up and get their day started. This, naturally, leads to a day full of distraction and slow movement.

People who are successful, and who rarely succumb to the grasp of procrastination, use this hour much differently. They wake up, maybe splash some water on their face, make themselves a drink and some breakfast, look over their agenda for the day, and possibly work in a quick exercise routine or at least get outside and get some fresh air. The exact routine will differ from person to person, but the general energy remains the same as they rise and get going right away. They may not be particularly quick during that first hour, but you can guarantee that they are not sitting around waiting until the last possible minute to get started. Even if they started slow, they still got up and got started. For the rest of the day, they carry that positive can-do energy with them everywhere they go, and their speed builds as they continue to work through the day. If you want to leverage power hour, you must do the same.

Leveraging Power Hour To The Fullest

Leveraging power hour to the fullest starts by creating a realistic and reasonable morning routine for you to follow. This routine needs to be quite different from the one you already follow, but, as you now know, it must create the same rewards that your current morning routine is already providing. If you are currently following a slow-to-rise morning routine, chances are your reward is that it conserves energy by being mindless, and it is comfortable. This means you need a morning routine that conserves energy by being mindless, and that is comfortable.

Your morning routine will become more mindless as it sinks into the habit level, but to help it get started, you can pick a morning routine that does not require a lot of thought or effort. Perhaps instead of waking up and exercising right away, you wake up and start a pot of coffee, then take your coffee outside and stand in the fresh air for a few minutes, without your cell phone so you can focus on waking up rather than distracting yourself. You can create the sensation of comfort by wearing comfortable clothing and standing in an area of your patio that feels comfortable, as well.

As you overcome procrastination and the many challenges relating to it, it is important that you do not self-sabotage by creating an unrealistic morning routine. Make it one that builds slow momentum at first because regardless of how slow that momentum is, it will still be effectively built-in that first hour of your day. As you begin to notice the positive impact of your power hour and grow used to this new habit, it will be easier for you to add more high-energy activities to that hour. Before you know it, you will be building massive amounts of momentum during that first hour, and procrastination will be a word of the past for you.

Revitalizing Your Energy As You Go

Your power hour will give you the best start to your day, but it is inevitable that at some point during the day, your momentum will start to dwindle. Especially if you have grown used to procrastination, you might find yourself quickly losing speed and falling back into a slump as early as mid-morning. It is important that you continue to leverage the theory of power hour to sustain your momentum as long as possible, as this will help you create stronger habits around your daily activities. This will also help that momentum grow day by day so that you can create even stronger results as the days go by.

A great way to revitalize your energy when it begins to slow down again is to recognize the slowing of your energy and engage in an activity that gradually builds your energy up. This is where many people will make a major mistake, though. That is, they engage in the "energy building" activity of taking a break, often by sitting down or otherwise giving themselves a chance to rest. Only, this does not create the type of momentum they need, because it contributes to lowered energy, not increased energy. A better option would be to engage in some light physical activity such as walking, stretching, or otherwise moving your body to gradually rebuild the energy within your body, which would effectively keep you going for the rest of the day. Many people falsely believe that by moving, they will drain the rest of their energy, but studies have proven that light physical exercise increases your energy, which is why it is advised to avoid nightly workouts and instead exercise in the morning.

The real reason you find yourself tired during the day often has less to do with physical tiredness and more to do with an overall disinterest in the activity at hand. It happens most often when you have been doing the same thing for too long, whether that be a specific activity, maintaining the same posture for too long, or anything else that could lead to physical, mental, and emotional boredom or exhaustion. By changing up your current state, either through switching your posture, switching your activity or both, you can quickly revitalize your energy and keep yourself going through the rest of the day. Next time you are at work, and you find yourself slowing down and struggling to stay focused, pause what you are doing, stand up, stretch your body, and count out ten deep breaths before sitting down and working again. If you can, hold a more intentional, healthy posture so you can keep yourself more mentally, emotionally, and physically engaged in the present task. That way, you overcome procrastination by increasing your energy, which will keep you going through the rest of the day.

Turning Todays Energy Into Tomorrow's Success

Your energy and momentum do not just build on a day to day basis; it builds continuously, too. This means that you are not just building your momentum over the hours of the day, but over the days themselves, too. The more you build today's energy and create positive momentum in your day, the better you will start off tomorrow, and the greater your positive momentum will be. At first, this may not be noticeable because the changes will be gradual, but as you continue to create positive momentum, you will find yourself experiencing continually increased momentum each day. Over time, maintaining your power hour and keeping your energy up during the day becomes easy because you have become accustomed to it. As they say, even a 1% improvement in your energy every day will lead to a 365% improvement in a year, so never discount the power of gradual change.

To understand the value of these positive day to day changes on your procrastination, you need to recall the fact that procrastination is motivated by negative feelings. This means that if you go into your day with negative momentum or slow energy, it becomes easier for you to procrastinate because you are already in a bad mood. As you continue to build positive momentum and sustain it throughout the day, you find yourself entering and experiencing each day from a more positive baseline of energy. This means you are already in a great mood, which means you are far less likely to procrastinate, and more likely to see your tasks through. Even crummy tasks that you cannot find a single way to enjoy will become less crummy because you are in a good mood overall, which means you are more resilient to the discomfort and willing to get them done.

Chapter 14: Setting Yourself Up For Success

Your current system is set up for failure, which is precisely why you have had so many troubles with overcoming procrastination in the past. Originally, your knowledge was inaccurate, your foundation was not strong, and you were consistently engaging in behaviors that encouraged, rather than discouraged, procrastination. Throughout the past 13 chapters, you have come to understand what procrastination actually is, what you must do to resolve procrastinating behaviors, and how you can permanently change your life. Now, you must discover how you can effectively embed these changed behaviors into a practical, everyday system that sets you up for success, rather than failure.

The Flaws Of Your Current System

Your current system is flawed. Everything you do feeds into instant gratification, easy rewards, and the ability to get yourself out of doing anything you do not want to be doing at the drop of a hat. You have become a mastermind at convincing yourself, and everyone else, that your procrastinating behaviors are fully justified and reasonable when, if you were to critically address them, you would realize they are nothing more than a waste of time. Maybe you already know that, too.

Still, your current system is flawed. It is full of habits and activities that set you up for failure by encouraging you to make the wrong choice. In fact, they make it way too easy for you to make the wrong choice, and that is why you keep making it. Don't believe me? Read this example and see how much of it you identify with. I'll bet you recognize many similarities between this and your own life. Or, at the very least, you could write something similar about yourself:

"You wake up in the morning, grab your phone, and scroll it to see what everyone is up to. Suddenly you realize you have to work in forty minutes, so you get up, drag your feet into the kitchen, and make yourself a coffee. As you drink the coffee, you keep reading that interesting post you had already started, and from there, you keep reading more posts while you attempt to get ready. You eat a small breakfast or pack something to eat on the way to work, quickly brush your teeth, throw on your clothes, and leave. At work, you head straight to the breakroom for another cup of coffee and stand around talking to the other procrastinators for as long as you can. After a while, the boss comes in for his coffee, and you scatter to make it appear as though you had been busy all along. When you sit at your desk, you scroll your phone some more, waiting until the very last minute to prepare for your upcoming appointment. This continues all day, even through your lunch break, because you didn't pack a lunch, since you had not given yourself enough time to do so. You have to prepare for a meeting you have been putting off, anyway, so it's not like you would have had time to eat in the first place. When work ends, you go home, drop onto the couch, and watch

TV until bedtime. At some point in between episodes, you convince yourself to get up and prepare a quick meal for yourself, but it never hits the spot. The next morning, you do it all over again."

Does this sound like you? If so, I'll bet that just by reading this excerpt, you can immediately witness several areas where you have effectively set yourself up for failure. The more you engage in those behaviors, the harder it is for you to make the right choice because you have made it so easy to make the wrong choice right from the start.

Routines To Avoid

The routines you must avoid include every single routine that makes it easy for you to make the wrong decision. Charging your phone on your nightstand, drinking your morning coffee on the couch, going into the breakroom when you first arrive at work, opening up distracting websites at your desk, and dropping onto the couch when you get home are bad routines. So are any other routines you partake in that reduce your energy or make it easy for you to distract yourself from what you should be doing.

A great way to get intimate with your schedule and understand the routines you, personally, need to be avoiding is to keep track of your daily routines for at least a week. Over that week, write down every routine you engage in, and what the result of that routine is, as this will help you understand where your routines are failing you. The routines that are making it too easy to make the wrong decision, or that are encouraging you to procrastinate are the very ones you need to avoid. You can avoid them by using the pivot method for shifting your habits in these areas of your life so that you can effectively pick up new habits that warrant stronger results.

A Successful Morning Routine

To help you get a better idea of how you can help yourself succeed, we are going to look over what a successful morning, afternoon, and evening routine should look like.

A successful morning routine would look like this:

- Your cell phone alarm wakes you up, and you have to walk across the room to turn it off and then immediately put your phone back down.

- You go to the bathroom, splash your face with some water or take a quick shower, then head into the kitchen.

- You make yourself a drink, start your breakfast, and stay standing the entire time. As your breakfast is being prepared, you prepare your lunch for work and take food out of the freezer for your dinner.

- When you are done eating, you take 5-10 minutes to engage in some form of physical activity that increases your energy. (Morning chores, walking the dog, or engaging in a quick exercise routine all count.)

- You get dressed, gather your items for work, and then head out the door to go about your day.

A Successful Afternoon Routine

A successful afternoon routine is something that should be easy to do around lunchtime every day, whether you are working or not. Keeping a quick, simple routine ensures that you can build your energy and your day to day momentum, regardless of what you are doing on that particular day.

A great example of a successful afternoon routine is:

- You prepare your lunch. As it is heating up, you engage in a 5-10 minute exercise routine. (Stretching, a short exercise routine, or physical errands all count. You could also take the stairs to the lunchroom if you are on a different floor from it.)

- You eat your lunch, give yourself three to five minutes to digest, and then immediately get up and clean up. You do not allow yourself to sit any longer than you need to.

- Before you get started on your next routine, you take 5-10 minutes to do some form of energizing activity that helps you break away from your regular routine. This could be talking to a friend, making a phone call, playing a game while standing up, reading a book, or doing anything that breaks you away from what you have been doing all day long.

- Go back to your daily tasks.

A Successful Evening Routine

A successful evening routine should help you wind down your energy while preparing for positive momentum the next day. This ensures that you do not go to bed wired and that you can start your next day off right.

A great evening routine would be:

- You eat dinner, then tidy up from your meal.

- You complete any outstanding chores for the day, so you don't have to put them on tomorrow's to-do list.

- You spend 20-30 minutes engaging in a relaxing activity. (Reading, bathing, meditating, or anything else low impact.)

- You set aside your clothes for the next day, set your alarm for the next morning, arrange your work items for the next day, and prepare yourself for the following morning in any way you prefer. (Set the coffee pot, prepare lunch for the next day, get your morning podcast ready to go, so you just hit play, etc.)

- You brush your teeth, comb your hair, wash your face, and get into bed.

- Before you fall asleep, you list 3-5 things you are grateful for and give yourself space to genuinely feel that gratitude so that you go to sleep feeling wonderful.

Chapter 15: Tracking And Reviewing Your Progress

Anytime you make a change in your life, you should always be ready to monitor that change to see how it is doing, and to see if you can do better in any areas relating to that change. Not monitoring your changes can lead to you reverting into old behaviors without realizing it, because falling back into old patterns is easier than maintaining new ones. Even long after you have made these changes, you might find yourself reverting due to an unexpected trigger or experience that sends you back into old habits. Regular tracking and reviewing of your changes, and mindfulness around your behaviors, ensure that you are not falling back into old, unwanted patterns.

With procrastination, it is important that you use your tracking and reviewing process mindfully to avoid using your tracking and reviewing as a way to procrastinate further. Understanding what is going on in your mind during these check-ins, and recognizing when you are obsessively checking in, will ensure that you are effectively monitoring your changes without doing so to the point of self-sabotage.

Why Check-Ins Become Counterproductive

Your brain is a highly efficient machine. When you decide to do something, your brain will regularly check in to ensure that you are doing it properly. For example, if you say you want to see every yellow car that passes you on your drive to the store, your brain will regularly check in with this information to ensure that you recall it, and that you check in enough to take action on that particular desire. When you *want* to check in on something, this is highly productive. When you do not want to be obsessively checking in, though, this is not productive. For example, let's say you are having an urge to do something distracting. If you try to push that thought out of your brain, you have given your brain the task to stop thinking about something. Your brain will now routinely check in on that thought to ensure you haven't been thinking about it, which will effectively bring it back into your thoughts and render it a failed attempt.

Instead of following this natural pattern, you need to find a more productive way to stop feeding into these urges, including the urge to obsessively check in on how you are doing with your productivity. You can do this by mindfully assigning your brain to a productive task, rather than one that can become counterproductive. For example, rather than checking in on whether or not you are procrastinating, you can check in on how productive you are being and how you can be more productive. This way, you are creating more productivity, and your check-ins are aiding that, rather than creating more distractions.

How To Have Productive Check-Ins

Productive check-ins are achieved during an active assignment by assigning your brain to a productive task. However, you will also need to have check-ins regarding your level of procrastination as well to ensure that you are experiencing improvements from your procrastinating tendencies. It is important to navigate these check-ins intentionally and mindfully to ensure that you are not wasting time by checking in too frequently.

The best way to have productivity check-ins is to specifically schedule a time where you will check in with your productivity and your procrastination. Write that time down in advance so you know when to expect it, and then commit to thinking only productive thoughts until then. Once your scheduled time has come, you can start to think about procrastination and how you have been doing through a more thorough check-in.

Your thorough check-in should happen entirely during the scheduled time, without distraction. You should have a method for what you are checking for, and you should follow that method every time. As soon as the scheduled time ends, you need to focus only on productive thoughts again. Do not allow yourself to become obsessed with checking and rechecking your thoughts, as this will lead to unproductive habits around your check-ins, which inevitably lead to more procrastination.

The easiest way to ensure that you are having productive check-ins is to schedule time daily, weekly, and monthly for your check-ins. Each day, you should give yourself about five minutes to check-in so you can reflect on how you are doing. Each week, give yourself about ten minutes to check-in and reflect on how you are doing, and each month give yourself about half an hour to check-in and reflect on how you are doing. This gives you plenty of time to reflect without overwhelming your schedule or feeding into your procrastination tendencies.

What You Need To Be Checking For

As you check for productivity and procrastination, you need to ensure that you are checking for the right things. What you want to be checking for is the habit loops surrounding your procrastination, what your distractions have been, how much time you have been investing in your distractions, and how effectively your coping methods have been working. Once you begin to check for one of these things, look at that aspect of your productivity thoroughly, and find a complete answer that you are satisfied with. Then, stop checking in on that particular part of your productivity and start checking in on something else.

It would be a good idea to write down your thoughts, opinions, and findings on all of these areas of your productivity in a journal so that you can keep track of them. This will help you have a more honest reflection of your history and how you have been doing with your productivity and procrastination. That way, you cannot bully yourself for doing worse than you actually have been, or encourage yourself to believe you are doing better than you have been. Instead, your findings are accurate, reflect reality, and can lead to even more productive changes in the future.

You should be doing three different levels of reflection on your efforts every time you research how you are doing. Your day to day check-ins should be surface level and should only reflect that specific day, while your weekly check-ins can reflect on the entire week, and your monthly check-ins can reflect on the past month and your entire history. By having strict levels of check-ins that you do with each individual check-in, you ensure that you are never distracting yourself with these check-ins and feeding into your procrastination.

Reinforcing Your Existing Strengths

As you do your check-ins, you will inevitably discover areas where you already have a relatively easy time breaking away from procrastination and focusing on what you are doing. These strengths are areas where you experience your fastest wins, and they are areas where you need to regularly check-in and reinforce them. When you are able to witness your strengths and reinforce them, you ensure that they continue to provide you the results you need to see tangible success from your efforts. These results show you how well you are doing at overcoming procrastination, which gives you the motivation and energy you need to resolve your weaknesses, too.

To reinforce your strengths, you want to recognize what they are and discover how you can leverage them even further. Always improve your strengths - the better you can do the further you will get. People who become complacent with their strengths will always find their strengths dwindling and that they have to work harder to improve their skills over and over again. Those who are aware of their strengths can continue to improve them, making it easier for their strengths to offset or improve their weaknesses.

With procrastination, your strengths may be anything from being excellent at putting your distractions down, to having incredible scheduling abilities. Your strengths may seem small or insignificant, but you will rapidly realize that they can be used to help you improve your results and quit procrastinating once and for all. For example, an excellent ability to put down your phone can be used to encourage yourself to take the very next step: stand up. Then, your excellent ability to put your phone down and standing up can turn into your ability to take the first step toward what needs to get done. You can continue building on these strengths until you are effectively reaching your desired results, every single time.

Strengthening Your Weaknesses

Like with everything, where you have strengths you will also have weaknesses. If you are not careful, it may seem like your weaknesses reduce the quality of your strengths, so you must always remember that your weaknesses mean nothing about what you can do. All they mean is that you have an area where you need to put extra effort into your skills so you can do a better job.

Before you can strengthen your weaknesses, you need to identify what they are in the first place. Your weaknesses are anything you seem to struggle with or struggle with more than you struggle with anything else. They are things that seem a little more challenging for you to come to terms with, and that makes it harder for you to create the results you desire. With procrastination, your weakness might be scrolling social media, sitting down when there is more to be done, or justifying the excuses you have created around why you have not yet started on an important task.

Once you know what your weaknesses are, you need to identify ways to use your strengths to offset those weaknesses, while also creating habits that will improve your weaknesses. For example, if scrolling social media is your weakness but you are excellent at putting your phone down, you can get into the habit of putting your phone down and leaving it alone between certain hours of the day. This way, social media isn't even an option because the device you use to access social media has been put down and put away.

You should regularly check in on your weaknesses and evaluate your coping methods to see how well you are doing with them. If you discover that your weaknesses are not improving or that your habits are not working, you need to come up with a new plan for how you will improve them. If you realize your approach is working, you can reflect on why it is working and use that information to help you improve your other areas of weakness, also.

Increasing Your Momentum And Success

Part of checking in is having the right mindset about your check-ins and using them to increase your momentum and success with overcoming procrastination. It can be easy to view your check-ins as an opportunity to see how bad you have been doing, or where you have been going wrong. You might intimidate yourself into believing that check-ins will only show you how terrible you have been and that they will be filled with self-loathing and self-punishment. It is important that you do not use that mindset when doing your check-ins, though, as doing so can lead to you sabotaging your results and destroying your success.

When you do your check-ins, start by elevating your mindset into one that has you curious about how well you have done, and about how much better you can do. With this mindset, you will have a much easier time creating positive momentum around your results, as you will be able to celebrate your wins and optimistically review the areas where you need improvement. This optimism will lead to hope, and this hope will lead to positive momentum.

You can also increase your momentum by asking yourself how much better you can do. Each time you review your procrastinating tendencies, do not just celebrate how well you have done, look for ways to do even better. This way, you are always strengthening your weaknesses and reinforcing your strengths, which leads to far greater outcomes. There is always room for improvement no matter how well you have done, and if you get into the habit of looking for those opportunities, you will create the ability to enjoy even more success in your pursuit of overcoming procrastination once and for all.

When Can You Stop Checking In?

If you have been dealing with a significant problem such as procrastination, you might find yourself wondering at what point you can stop checking in. It can be easy to convince yourself that if you have been doing well for any period of time, it is time for you to stop checking in. Unfortunately, many people believe that the great results they experience early on are evidence that they were not struggling as much as they were, so they stop checking in almost right away. This leads to them reverting to old behaviors and struggling to get back on track.

Eventually, you will not have to check in nearly as often, but for the time being it is important that you have your daily, weekly, and monthly check-ins. You will know you are ready to reduce your check-ins when you have effectively moved through the "stages of change." The stages of change come in three stages: the novelty, the blah, and the normal. The novelty stage is the part where your change is new, exciting, and interesting. Because it is so different from what you are used to, you have fun fulfilling those changes, and you may even become cocky about how well you are doing. If you are at this point, you will know it because it seems like everything is magically better, and it wasn't so hard after all.

The blah stage is the part where you start to experience regression and find yourself not wanting to partake in the changes anymore. Old habits may try to sink in, triggers may seem harder to overcome, and you might find yourself excessively justifying unwanted habits. During this stage, you need to rely on the habits you made in the novelty stage to help you continue to uphold your changed behaviors.

The final stage, the normal stage, is characterized by you moving beyond the struggle of upholding your new habits on a day to day basis and finding that they feel normal. It takes quite a while for this stage to fully set in. Once it truly has, though, you want to give yourself several more weeks of check-ins to ensure that you are truly there and nothing regresses. Then, you can start reducing your check-ins to only a few times a month as an opportunity to ensure that you are not regressing. You may also intentionally plan check-ins around known triggers that you will be facing so that you can be more attentive to your needs during those times. When you have reached this point, you know you have had great success with overcoming procrastination!

Conclusion

Congratulations on completing *Uninstall Procrastination!* I know, it's a lot to take in and if you have gotten this far then, you're already ahead of most people who've picked up this book but procrastinated on actually reading it. It's a good reason to feel proud of yourself, but don't stop here - the real work has just begun. The real work is your dreams and your goals, and I hope that you have found something in this book that can help you achieve them.

In closing, I wanted to touch upon a few more things - bear with me, please.

The idea for "Uninstall Procrastination" came to me when I realized that we are all equipped with the same operating system (OS). This OS is the same system that motivates us to do things, and it also motivates us to not do things. The difference is in the software that is installed on top of it.

That's right, the same reward processes that motivate us to take action also can motivate us to procrastinate. And sometimes it is O.K. to procrastinate - sometimes there are good reasons to delay doing something. However, it is up to us to decide when we need to delay and when we need to take action. The challenge with that is, our brain is primarily concerned with our survival, and when those basic needs are met, it is more concerned with preserving energy than motivating us to do anything remotely challenging and not related to our immediate survival. That is why it is so hard to get off the comfort of your couch and get to work when you're well-fed, warm, and entertained - as far as your brain is concerned - you're doing great. It's even more challenging in our age of infinite entertainment on demand. It's something our forefathers did not have to deal with - all the Netflix, video games, social media, etc. We have to be vigilant about how we choose to spend our time more than ever.

So, how do you uninstall procrastination software and install a more productive one?

You have to make it your goal to strategically train yourself to move away from easy, instant rewards and comfort, and move toward doing more challenging activities, embrace discomfort and delay gratification. Use the tools described in this book to help you along your path to self-mastery. The more you train your brain to enjoy challenging work the more used to it it's going to become and with time, the motivation to do harder tasks will come easier and easier. Don't give up!

There will be times when despite your best efforts, you're just not going to feel like it. There will be times when all your clever tricks and strategies won't change the way you feel. You might try to fight it with logic and reason but allow me to suggest a different approach. If you don't feel like it, just admit it. Be honest with yourself and admit that you don't want to do what you intended and that it's fine - be understanding, forgive yourself if you feel guilty.

Say, you come home after work and intend to go to the gym but now you feel tired and just not that into the idea anymore. Accept that you feel like that and don't fight the feeling, instead ask yourself - can I still go to the gym, even if I feel tired? Can I still do it even when I don't feel like doing it?

If there's nothing physically stopping you and it's just a feeling, you will realize that you can still do it even if you don't feel like it. The more often you can become aware of this and make yourself take action when you don't feel like it, the stronger your anti-procrastination software is going to become.

I know it sounds simplistic - "Sometimes you just gotta do it" but sometimes that's all there is to it.

Most of the strategies in this book are going to help you feel more "like it" but there will be times like I mentioned when you will not feel "like it" and that's when you have to realize that you don't need to rely on your feelings to start taking action.

Don't fight the feeling, acknowledge it, and just get on with the work.

The difference between people who are successful and those who procrastinate is not that they are somehow impervious to procrastination (remember we all have the same OS), it's that they are better at dealing with that impulse - they are running better software. Now, you can be one of those successful people.

It's going to take some time so be patient with yourself. If you put in the effort to stay consistent, results will come. Check-in with yourself regularly to make sure you stay on track and try to have some fun with it. After all, you are working towards achieving your goals and building a better life for yourself and your loved ones, it should feel exciting.

Lastly, if you can please take a moment to review *Uninstall Procrastination: How to Beat Chronic Procrastination and Get things Done* on Amazon Kindle, I would appreciate it. Your honest review helps others who are searching for this very knowledge discover it, so they too can overcome their procrastinating behaviors and become more productive.

Thank you, and best of luck!

Printed in Great Britain
by Amazon